MIRACLE
Facing the Challenge of Jesus

The Greatest Miracle

by Melvin Banks
with Jenny Roberts

author of

Healing Revolution
Healing Secrets
Radiant Christian Living

Forthcoming title by Melvin Banks:

Keeping Alive. . . All Through Life, a sequel to *Radiant Christian Living*. Melvin Banks draws on his thirty-five years as a minister and evangelist to pursue a number of themes including; winning over stress; how to unlock your faith-power; the meanings of love, patience and wisdom; and secrets of a dynamic new life.

Rev. Melvin Banks would be pleased to hear from readers. Please write to him at:

Crusade Office
44 Monk's Way
Cricketts Meadow
Chippenham
Wilts
SN15 3TT

(Please send s.a.e.)

Tel. 0249–655712

The GREATEST MIRACLE

Facing the Challenge of Jesus

MELVIN BANKS

with
Jenny Roberts

Marshall Pickering

Marshall Morgan and Scott
Marshall Pickering
3 Beggarwood Lane, Basingstoke, Hants RG23 7LP,
UK

First published in 1988 by Marshall Morgan and Scott
Publications Ltd
Part of the Marshall Pickering Holdings Group
A subsidiary of the Zondervan Corporation

British Library Cataloguing in Publication Data

Banks, Melvin
    The greatest miracle.
    1. Jesus Christ
    I. Title
    232

    ISBN 0–551–01646–9

Text set in 10/11pt Linotron Baskerville by
Input Typesetting Ltd., Wimbledon SW19 8DR
Printed in Great Britain by Cox and Wyman, Reading

Contents

Dedication
To my precious wife and partner Lilian who, like myself, not only believes in miracles but testifies, by the living Christ, that we are a miracle, through his unmerited favour and grace.

Acknowledgements
To my ever-growing team, including John, Brian, Roland, Chris, Dave, Sue, Maurice and Christine, Philip and Paul, Jim, Jolliffe, and Margaret. Also to our many helpers, including George, Mrs Newby, Miss Howitt, the Simons family of Bedford, the Prices of Gorseinon, Ernie and Anne, Miss Sedman, Mr Waterhouse, the Pimlotts of Norwich, David Hussey, and of course, June our typist.

Introduction

George Bernard Shaw, the famous playwright, said when nearing the end of his life:

> The world is full of miracles . . . the man who denies their existence is a man who is wrong in his definition of a miracle. Some miracles are credible, some are incredible . . . the man who will not believe this, and who won't feel the truth of this, will not believe anything.

G. K. Chesterton, the poet and essayist, said:

> We are gorged daily by unquestionable miracles . . . it is ridiculous for us to make a difficulty about believing this or that merely because it is a miracle . . . I am prepared to accept all the miracles of religious record.

Robert Ingersoll, a sceptic and agnostic, said:

> Show me the signs and wonders and miracles of the Bible . . . and I will believe in Christianity.

Paul, the apostle, said:

> God bearing them witness, both with signs and wonders, and with different miracles, and gifts of the Holy Ghost (Heb. 2:4)

1: Miracles

'If ever you needed a miracle it is today,' said the raw-faced, solemn New Zealander, as he negotiated the early morning rush hour traffic of Auckland's suburbia. I sat silent as he continued, 'We are really up against it today, Melvin. Nothing like this has ever been attempted on the media here.'

I gulped an acknowledgement, feeling rather like an innocent victim pressed into taking someone else's place on the guillotine! A car horn beeped behind us; an ambulance siren wailed in the distance, taking some casualty case to hospital. I might be a casualty myself by the end of the morning, I reflected nervously.

I had arrived for my first visit to New Zealand only three days before, brought by the faith and inspiration of one pastor and one church of 150 people. My ministry was quite unknown in this country. Through the car window I watched as the colonial-style wooden buildings of the suburbs gave way to the shining glass and tower blocks of the city. Auckland, while perhaps not as vast as other great cities of the world, was nevertheless, as I had learned, a needy city. I had prayed for it much in recent months as, while I travelled through England, my thoughts had turned to my forthcoming visit to this beautiful country. Now I needed prayer more than ever before.

I had made an urgent call to Brian Hilliard, my British crusade organiser, and Keith Simons, my secretary, asking them to pray and to organise all the intercession for me that they could, back in Britain. Although I had been warned of this impending confrontation just before I had left England, I had not realised just what I was letting myself in for. After the first meetings of the campaign, which had attracted good-size congregations, Pastor John Coleman had explained to me the challenge that lay ahead of us.

The Radio Pacific station had made New Zealand media history by inviting us to pray publicly for the healing of the sick. Some weeks before, they had issued an announcement inviting any sick and incurable people, willing to come onto the programme to be prayed for by the English evangelist, to apply to them. They were overwhelmed by the response and, from the huge number of applications, eventually chose five very sick people.

The station authorities were well aware of the genuine sickness of the people selected, and the idea was that I should not meet them until the actual programme, which was to go out 'live'. They had announced that I would be laying hands on these people, and had used phrases like 'to see if it's genuine' and 'if there's anything in it'. So I knew I was facing a barrage of scepticism and, as I walked through the swing doors of Radio Pacific, I felt like Daniel going into the lions' den!

I had not boasted of my ministry; I had not claimed to be a 'healer'; I had never, at any time, claimed to do anything in my own power. However, the reputation I had gained in over 30 years of ministry in Britain was enough to make me a target for sceptics, eager to expose anything about my ministry that was not genuine. The people at the radio station did not believe in my ministry, and I knew that they hoped to catch me out and prove that I could not produce the goods. They were not dishonest or corrupt people, but were approaching the issue in the only way that their unregenerate minds then knew.

As I shook hands with the producer, his assistant, the technicians, and the interviewer, I caught out of the corner of my eye the winks, the smirks, and a hint of expectation of a good time at my expense. But as I sat waiting to go on, praying quietly in tongues, the Spirit of the Lord arose in my being with an anointing such as I had not felt for many years.

Although I must have been praying only for moments, I was so lost in God that it seemed like an age, and I was quite oblivious to all that was taking place around me. I was brought back to earth with the noise of a door shutting and a voice saying, 'Coffee, Reverend Banks?'

'Pardon?'

'Coffee . . . oh, are you all right?'

'Yes, I'm all right. No coffee thanks.'

'We're ready for you now,' said the assistant, and my thoughts flew to my darling wife Lilian, who was fasting and praying in our lodgings at the other end of the city. Pastor Coleman told me later that many pastors were listening all around Auckland, and in one church four pastors sat huddled around the set awaiting the annihilation of this funny little Englishman who had dared to 'take on the NZ broadcasting set-up'. There were some who had said that I was crazy to presume on God and risk the good name of the evangelical Church in the country, and put so much at stake. It was just as well I did not know all that was being said about me as New Zealand's most popular morning programme, broadcast from end to end of the two islands, was about to begin.

I made myself comfortable in the chair opposite the interviewer, eyeing through the glass panelling the engineers turning knobs, the producer and two others on

11

the programme's staff walking around, shuffling papers, talking. The red light came on.

'This is Radio Pacific; this is the moment you have all been waiting for. We have here in our studios the healing evangelist from the United Kingdom, the Reverend Melvin Banks, on his first visit to New Zealand, and holding healing services in Glendene, here in Auckland. We also have in the studio...' and he announced the names of the five people, each incurable, each given up by the medical world, who they were challenging me to 'heal'.

I felt humbled and quietened, but in my heart came a voice: 'The Kingdom of God is within you. Preach the gospel of the Kingdom and heal the sick. My Kingdom is in you; my power is in you; *it is not you, but I* who will defend my word. I will work such a work that many will wonder... remember you have the power of the Kingdom *in you!*' I felt such confidence, such boldness arising in me. The anointing was upon me; I was the King's representative, the ambassador of the King of Kings!

The first of the sick people entered. She looked so pathetic and needy. She was crippled in her shoulders and spine, paralysed by arthritis and a form of spondylitis. She was racked with pain and her body had been seized up for 14 years.

I laid hands on her and prayed. I felt power surging into her beyond myself. She began to cry out, 'Oh, it's wonderful! It's wonderful! Look at that!' and she sat up, moved her shoulders briskly, and bent her spine. Then she was dancing round the studio! She could bend; she could jump; her rigid neck was free; all her pain had disappeared; she could do the impossible.

The interviewer began to get very excited as he delivered his commentary. 'We know all about this woman.

She has not moved like this for 14 years! Mr Banks has never met her before – this is amazing!'

Then one after the other the sick people were brought in, and God healed four of them. The fifth, though not healed, was greatly helped and comforted and felt some improvement, so was also very joyful. The studio became like the scene of a revival meeting. People were praising God, the staff were visibly flabbergasted, the switchboard was jammed with telephone calls, and people began to arrive at the studio wanting prayer. Announcements were hastily made: 'Please do not come to the studio, but go to see the evangelist at the big marquee in Glendene.'

Then one of the studio staff came in. This was an associate producer who had previously rejected totally the idea of Christ's healing power. Now he came to ask me if I would pray for him. He had pulled a muscle 18 months before, and had suffered ever since from constant, nagging pain, which no medical help had been able to alleviate. I laid hands on him and he too was instantly and miraculously healed – and all this broadcast 'live' from the studio! At last, after a gruelling three-hour session of answering phone-in calls, responding to the interviewer's questions, praying, and seeing miracles, I left the studio on the best possible terms with the station staff, and with hundreds of thousands of newly-made sympathisers from all over New Zealand.

At our public meetings the crowds grew to 1,000 nightly in the tent, and when an overflow system was organised, we were seeing congregations of 1,500. We had to move to a huge church building in the city centre as the crowds continued to grow and grow, until thousands had been reached with the gospel of Christ. The same happened in the other cities we visited: Christchurch, Wellington, Whangarei. Crowds packed the largest halls; in a month some 4,000 came to Christ, and 10,000 came forward for healing prayer. Amazing miracles of supernatural healing were seen! Pastor John Coleman said, 'It touched every part of our nation of New Zealand, with dynamic effect on the non-church-going public . . . not seen here for 60 years since the visit of the old healing evangelists Valdez and Smith Wigglesworth; thousands healed, vast numbers turned to Christ.'

C S Lewis defined a miracle as 'an interference with nature by supernatural power.' It is the unique act of God, the supernatural activity of God. I have seen miracle after miracle: incredible miracles, extraordinary miracles, stunning miracles! I have seen the conquest of debilitating diseases; the beds of the sick and the paralysed emptied; I have even seen a dead person raised – God-ordained miracles, God-executed miracles!

I sometimes drive through a little town in Lincolnshire where I held one of my first crusades. God had swept in with revival power, and a church was established. I pass what was clearly once a pre-war style cinema, but is now a supermarket, and every time I pass I say to myself: there is a testimony to the miracles of God today. What had happened was that during my ministry there, the cinema owner was saved and she became a strong disciple of Christ. This was 18 years ago, when the cinema was much more popular than it is now, but that woman decided to close her cinema down so that films of questionable morality would no longer be shown in the area. The town became a healthier and happier place, bearing witness to God's good work today. *That was a miracle of God! His supernatural power moving in revival closed that cinema down!*

St Augustine said, 'I should not be a Christian but

for the miracles.' Miracles evoke wonder, awe, and even the fear of Almighty God. Miracles demonstrate the explosive power of the Almighty!

A short time ago I held a healing service in a Northamptonshire town. At the afternoon service the crowds were enormous, packing the hall so densely that we could not squeeze one more person in. They were crammed into every corner of the building; they sat in the side rooms, the kitchen, the aisles. We could not even stand to sing! A woman had brought her profoundly deaf granddaughter for prayer, but they could not get in, so they stood outside the hall all through the service. She later testified that, as I was praying for the sick, she felt a sense of awe, wonder, and divine glow. A flow of power seemed to shoot through the building, and at that moment the child began to clutch its ears tightly. She could hear the traffic on the main road; she could hear the praise and clapping of the people in the hall. Since then hospitals have testified to her healing: *that was a miracle!*

The Oxford Dictionary defines a miracle as: 'anything beyond human power and deviating from common action of the laws of nature.' A. M. Hunter says that if a person '. . . is dominated by a spirit, miracles are possible; if by a spirit of love it is probable.' Even the agnostic George Bernard Shaw believed in miracles: 'we are gorged daily by them,' he said.

We have an amazing God, an amazing Jesus, an amazing Saviour and healer! I can bring to mind so many examples of his miraculous power. I was recently touring the West Country, visiting new churches which I had seen planted during my ministry there over the past few years. One wet and blustery Sunday afternoon, between large morning and evening meetings, I squeezed in a visit to a small church in a village near the coast. There were about 50 people in the congregation, and during the service ten people gave their hearts to the Lord, which was most encouraging for this small fellowship.

At the end of the service I prayed for the sick then, after shaking hands with people and drinking a quick cup of tea, I was heading for the door. One of the local leaders stopped me. 'Do you know who was converted today?'

'What do you mean,' I asked, not knowing what to expect.

'Today,' he told me, 'one of the great train robbers came to Christ.'

I caught my breath as I remembered the notorious robbery of the Royal Mail in Buckinghamshire in 1963. This man, it appeared, had been one of the ringleaders. He had been in prison for many years, and had become asthmatic. He had now come along to the church, 'to give it a try', and had found Christ. He also had a wonderful release from his asthma. *That was a miracle!*

Then there is my friend Bert in Portsmouth: a living testimony to the miraculous power of Christ today. Bert was a heavy drinker; he spent his days in the pub and believed in nothing – not even in himself. One evening his wife announced that she was going out. Bert was puzzled as she tended to be a homebird who rarely went out by herself, but his wife explained about the leaflet that came through the door, and that she wanted to see the evangelist and be prayed for. Bert laughed and went off to the pub, but when he arrived home that night he found his wife joyful and singing hymns.

The same thing happened every night that week. Bert was mystified by the change in his wife, yet he resisted all her attempts to persuade him to come to a meeting. At last the crusade ended and I moved on to another town. But Bert's wife had bought one of the tapes that were on sale at the crusade, a tape of Alan Pimlott, the renowned soloist from Norwich. She played this wonderful tape almost nonstop. Bert heard it when he got up in the morning; he heard it when he came home from the pub each night. Finally he was touched by it. Two of the elders from the local Christian Fellowship prayed for Bert and he was converted. A lifetime's habit of heavy drinking stopped immediately; he was set free!

I often see Bert when I preach in Portsmouth: a short, well-built man singing lustily with the Langstone Fellowship singers – a witness of the change wrought by the risen Christ, *a modern miracle of Christ Jesus our Lord!*

I have this confirmation of the miraculous from a respected doctor, Dr Q. M. Adams MRCS LRCP FRSM:

I have attended Rev. Melvin Banks's missions on several occasions, indeed some of my own patients, including a young farmer's wife, have been amazingly cured. This particular person, whose condition I knew well, was suffering greatly from a spinal condition which was deteriorating despite all my efforts. After Rev. Banks's laying on of hands and prayers she was astonishingly and instanteously healed, and has never suffered since. She can now run, jump, and lie down painlessly. There are others I know of who were also cured completely. I have personally checked many cases and am aware of the genuine illnesses of many of the people who have visited Mr Banks. There are, without doubt, many miracles in his services.

I sat in a crowded chapel in Cornwall not long ago, and saw a blind man led in. On investigating the case I discovered that the man had been blind for at least eight years, and had travelled 80 miles, over remote country roads, to get to the service. Later in the meeting, as crippled people were seen joyfully and painlessly walking, and deaf people regained their hearing, this man started to describe the cross on the far end of the wall of the chapel, the height of the windows, the colours of the flowers decorating the church. *It was without doubt all real and genuine.*

I was holding a mission a few years ago in a town in the north of England. Some five newspapers reported the sensational scenes that took place. The local bingo hall manageress was quoted as saying, 'I may as well close up; I have done virtually no business this last two weeks.' Police had to be called out to control the traffic, for crowds of people were travelling to the services as news of the miracles spread. This was a mining community hard hit by the recession and with a very low rate of churchgoing; these were tough, sceptical, unemotional people. *That was a miracle for today!*

In another town people pulled off the church gates to get in, and climbed the scaffolding around the church to look through the windows. In Gloucester people stood in pouring rain for three hours, sat in the windows, stood outside and crammed the doorways in their eagerness to hear the message we were bringing.

In a small Chinese town near Kuala Lumpur people slept on the streets where a meeting was to take place; queued up for two days; 2,000 packed a cinema seating 700, and an estimated 3,000 stood outside. *That was revival blessing! That was a miracle!*

Again in Malaysia, I was staying in a small house in a jungle area. There were hard wooden beds, no carpets on the floor, no bath or shower, and I was tormented with mosquito bites. It was certainly tough going, but God was blessing in divine visitation. Huge halls in the

18

jungle villages and towns had been packed, and we had seen great miracles.

One day the old black telephone began to ring, on and off, squeaking and coughing, as though it were at its last gasp! The pastor's voice was faint, even though it was coming from only a few miles away. Although there had been meetings every night, he was calling to tell me that the service scheduled for four days ahead had been cancelled by the police. In that Muslim country it is against the law to hold a Christian meeting outside a church. Open air meetings are banned and meetings in public halls or cinemas need a permit and special police permission, which is often withheld. Apparently no reason had been given for withdrawing permission in this case.

I phoned the police station and spoke to one officer after another. All had different excuses: the form had been lost; the form had been filled in with the name of a different hall, not the large one we had intended to use. Could they not just change the name of the hall on the form, I asked. But no, a new form had to be filled in, and it would take a month for permission to be granted – and the crusade only had three more weeks to run! When the pastor arrived I had finally given up and was slumped in a chair. The young Chinese pastor was despairing. 'We cannot hold the meeting; you will be arrested and deported and the wonderful crusade will come to an end. There are three more weeks to go and town after town is awaiting your visit!'

I took a deep breath and swatted a mosquito. 'Let's pray about it,' I said.

'But it is impossible,' the pastor replied. It was clear that he was used to this kind of thing and had grown resigned to it.

Three days later I was reading the English-language

Muslim daily newspaper, and read that the following day the new King of Malaysia was to be crowned in the capital of Kuala Lumpur. Suddenly God's inspiration struck me and I paced the room in excitement, muttering 'I've got it! I've got it!' I picked up the phone and asked for the police station. When I finally got through to the assistant chief inspector I reminded him about the hall which we had hoped to use the following day.

'I am going to report you to the authorities in Kuala Lumpur,' I told him. 'Tomorrow is the King's coronation and we want to hold a great prayer meeting for your royal family. You are denying your people, and my fellow-Christians, their basic human rights as citizens of this country. We will certainly report you for denying religious freedom for the citizens of this area to pray for their king.'

There was silence for a moment, then a half apology, and then, 'But you are not Muslims,' he said.

'That makes no difference. The Bible teaches us to pray for kings and all those who have authority over us. We respect authority but you have shown no respect for those who want to pray for their rulers.'

We carried on endlessly in this way until finally the officer told me to leave it with him; he would ring back. I relaxed, feeling peaceful and confident, and within the hour the phone had rung. It was the chief superintendent, most apologetic, and confirming police permission for us to hold our meeting.

The following evening I arrived to find crowds of people cramming every available space in the hall; nearly the entire population of the village and surrounding areas had come. A row of police officers stood at the back watching, while the pastors sat with me, in some anxiety that all would be well. I prayed for the royal family, possibly the longest prayer I have ever prayed. When I looked up the police were leaving, presumably satisfied. I went on to preach; hundreds responded to the gospel appeal and many were healed. *Only a miracle could have changed the minds of those Muslim authorities!*

Why does God work miracles? Why did Jesus work miracles in his earthly ministry? Let us look at some of the reasons.

They Are Proof Of Christ's Deity And Relationship With The Father

Jesus refused to perform miracles as a sign, except for what he called the 'sign of Jonah', referring to his death and resurrection (Matt. 12:38-41). He never used his miracles to gratify people's fleeting desire for sensation. But to the serious seeker who was desperately needing proof, like John the Baptist in Luke 7:20-22, he pointed to his miracles as a seal of his authority and proof of his deity. The miracles were proof to John that Jesus was the promised Messiah. *Should they not be sufficient for us?* They were proof for Nicodemus in John 3:2, '. . . no man can do these miracles that thou doest, except God be with him.' Again, Jesus told the demon-possessed man who he had delivered (Mark 5:19) to go and tell his friends the 'great things the Lord had done' for him. The blind man who Jesus healed at the pool of Siloam told his questioners, 'Never since the world began has it been heard that anyone opened the eyes of a man born blind. If this man were not from God, he could do nothing' (John 9:32-33).

A 70-year-old woman, born blind, came for prayer to one of my Lancashire crusades. After prayer she could see the windows of the church, and could count fingers. Within six months she could see quite clearly and was interviewed on television, appearing to millions of people at peak viewing time. *'Jesus Christ is the same yesterday and today and for ever'* (Heb. 13:8). In Acts 2:22 Peter preached the proof of Christ's messiahship: 'Jesus of Nazareth, a man approved of God, among you by miracles and signs and wonders, which God did by him in the midst of you.'

Alan Richardson has said, 'In all the Gospels, Jesus is unwilling to work miracles as mere displays . . . in the Synoptic Gospels and in St John the miracles are evidence (of) who Jesus is . . . this, we shall maintain, is their *raison d'tre* in all four Gospels'. F B Meyer comments: 'the phrase *works of God* is a familiar one throughout the Gospel . . . they were the signs and seals of his mission'.

Jesus says in John 15:24 'If I had not done among them the works which no one else did, they would not have sin.' People saw their own sinfulness, they saw themselves as they really were against the miraculous revelation of the divine and supernatural being of God in Christ. The miracles of Christ forced the message of God onto people. And it is still the case that without miracles there is little salvation; without the revelation of the supernatural Jesus there is no spiritual impact on a community. *We need signs, wonders, and miracles to win people.*

W P F Burton, the great Congo missionary, who pioneered over 1,000 churches through his apostolic work said, 'The miraculous works of Christ were his credentials.' My good friend Pastor Percy Brewster, who established some 50 churches in Britain in his lifetime, said, 'Miracles are the badge of authority . . . given to us by the Father.' Harold Horton said, 'Miracles are the golden bow that in God's purpose fling the arrow of the gospel.' Jesus himself said, 'Believe me that I am in the

22

Father, and the Father in me, or else believe me for the very works' sake' (John 14:11).

Christ Worked Miracles Out Of His Compassion

Jesus gave us his brief right at the start of his earthly mission when, in Luke 4:18 he quoted Isaiah 61:

> The spirit of the Lord is upon me, because he hath anointed me to preach the gospel to the poor; he hath sent me to heal the broken-hearted, to preach deliverance to the captives, and recovering of sight to the blind, to set at liberty them that are bruised . . .

He went on to say that the scripture had been fulfilled that day.

The word that is translated as *compassion* in the Greek literally means 'to have the bowels of yearning' or 'deep earnest heart yearning'. There are also implications of 'being moved with an indescribable longing' and 'full of tenderness and desire to help'; all this speaks of God and reveals his loving heart. The Greek verb *splagchnizomai* refers to the kind of emotion of a father when his prodigal son returns home.

Francis McNutt said, 'His healing shows the strength of his compassion for the sick.' Compassion was a stronger motive than the need to prove his mission. The Gospels contain some 11 references to the compassion of Christ.

He Worked Miracles To Relieve Humanity

As Jesus mingled with people he was stirred by their needs, and in meeting those needs sought no personal publicity. He was concerned with each person who confronted him, seeing them as individuals.

One of the hallmarks of my ministry, and one which has often been highlighted by the press, is the personal interest shown to each sick person by our team. It has been commented that 'personal prayer and interest is shown to each and every one at every single service.' I always take this as a high commendation. In a world where people are treated so often as mere numbers on computer files, God treats us as individuals!

I was campaigning a few years ago in a large town in France; around 1,500 people were coming each day to the meetings. A young woman carried her son to the hall; he had a growth on his knee, he could not even stand, and amputation was a possibility. Two weeks later the boy was running about on the platform in front of cheering crowds as his mother described how he had been cleared by the hospital as completely cured.

I think of little David in Reading. When I was asked to pray for him he was unable to walk; he pulled himself around on his stomach; there were no nerves in his legs, and the hospital had said he would never walk. Within three months of that prayer he was standing, and within a month walking. He is now a completely normal, fit and healthy teenager.

Mrs Elley of Maidstone had spent many years in a wheelchair. She came, as a sceptic, to one of our services, and we prayed for her in the name of Jesus. From that day she could walk perfectly, and is now able to lead a normal, active life.

These miracles, and the many, many more that I have

seen in 25 years of ministry, demonstrate to me God's interest in the individual – his concern to deliver humanity!

It is interesting to note that Christ actually spoke very little about healing itself. Although so much of the Gospel accounts describe his healing works, his words are almost entirely concerned with redemption. Yet when he saw sickness and suffering he healed it. Though healing the sick was so important it was, nevertheless, supplementary; it was secondary to salvation.

Jesus said first, 'thy sins be forgiven thee'; then 'arise . . . and walk' (Mark 2:2-12).

David said first, 'who forgiveth all thine iniquities'; then 'who healeth all thy diseases' (Ps. 103:3).

God said, through Moses, 'if thou will . . . hearken to the voice of the Lord thy God, and wilt do that which is right in his sight . . . I will put none of these diseases upon thee . . . for *I am the Lord that healeth thee*' (Ex. 15:26).

Healing miracles are an extra, yet a vital part of God's message.

He Worked Miracles To Show The Way For The Church

Jesus said, 'the works that I do, ye shall do also' (John 14:12); 'they shall lay hands on the sick and they shall recover' (Mark 16:18); 'whatsoever city ye enter . . . heal the sick that are therein' (Luke 10:8,9). The Lord's message to the Church was clear, but sadly he has been let down by much of the Church through history.

A minister once told me that, just before I arrived for a well-planned mission, one of his congregation had said, 'I hope nothing supernatural is going to happen in the church when this Rev. Banks comes'! How sad – and what ignorance! *The Church is supernatural; Christ's body is miraculous; his special people are a living miracle!*

The miraculous covers many areas, not only healing of the body. I know that, in my own ministry, establishing 40 churches has been miraculous. It is a miracle to establish just one church! To bring together people of diverse backgrounds to live harmoniously with one another, to love one another, and share with one another, is a miracle and a supernatural act. To forgive and be forgiven is a miracle. As Alexander Pope said, 'to err is human, to forgive, divine.' To be filled with the Holy Spirit and speak with a beautiful unknown tongue is divine. To build the Church of God and see all its needs met – financial, spiritual, practical – is supernatural. Hudson Taylor once said: 'There are three stages to the work of God: one, it is impossible; two, it is difficult; three, it's done!'

Many people have no concept of a divine God. There was once a performance of Handel's *Messiah* where a misprint had crept into the programme. Instead of saying, 'the Lord God omnipotent reigneth', it read, 'the Lord God omnipotent resigneth'! And that's true of many people's God. To them the God of miracles has given up.

Without miracles there is no gospel. Without the supernatural, faith has no foundation or life. Miracles are God's normal way of healing and his only way of deliverance. A non-miraculous God is as helpless as we are, except as a moral example. But miracles, through the supernatural gifts of the Spirit, can make us God-like. Without the supernatural the New Testament becomes a harder legalistic system even than the law of Moses, and grace is dead. Every miracle of God is proof that his grace is unmerited and unaided, and *God expects his body to produce miracles today!*

He Worked Miracles To Teach His Precepts And Principles

The Holy Spirit lights up his word, and teaches us many things from Christ's miracles. They are not just demonstrations of his power, or evidence of his messiahship, or his compassion. What we learn from Christ's miracles and his personal contact with people in these incidents can stimulate our faith.

So much of the Gospel narratives relate to miracles. In the first ten chapters of Mark, for example, 200 out of 425 verses deal directly with miracles. Alan Richardson said, 'they are truly heavenly stories with an earthly meaning.' Dr Martin Lloyd Jones said, 'All of our Lord's miracles are more than events, they are parables as well . . . that does not mean we do not believe in the actual fact of them.' The whole point of the miracles is to awaken saving faith in the person of Christ as the Word of God. John tells us, 'many other signs truly did Jesus in the presence of his disciples . . . that ye might believe that Jesus is the Christ, the Son of God; and that *believing ye might have life through his name.*'

In The Miracles We See God's Ingenuity And Diversity

What amazing diversity we see in Christ's miracles. He speaks just a word to a Roman centurion and his servant is healed; yet the Syrophenician woman had to beseech him for help, until at last he delivered her demon-possessed child. He travels to Bethany to raise Lazarus from the dead; he lets a woman push through the crowd to pull at his garment before he heals her. One day he heals the sick by the laying-on of hands; another day he uses spit and clay to heal a blind man. One day he heals with a touch, a word, a look; the next he says that only those who returned to give thanks were made whole. Wonderful Jesus – always so original! Marvel beyond marvel, wonder beyond wonder, glorious beyond glorious is He!

Besides Christ's miracles of healing and deliverance we have the miracle of the water changed to wine, his walking on the water, the loaves and fishes, the cursing of the fig tree, and so many more. And the miracles continued under the apostles, with supernatural events like Peter's miraculous release from prison, Paul's raising of Eutychus, the deliverance of Paul and 276 others from shipwreck, besides countless miracles of physical healing.

God's diversity is seen too in the Old Testament miracles. There are many well-known miracles of healing, such as the healing of Miriam from leprosy and Elijah's raising of the widow's son, as well as supernatural events like the parting of the Red Sea and the manna that appeared day after day for 40 years. But there are also many interesting and almost forgotten miracles in the Bible. These reveal to us a many-splendoured God – a God so diverse, so unlimited that we cannot bind him with our traditions. Let us look at some of these more unusual or obscure miracles.

1. The miracle of the clothes and shoes of the children of Israel which did not wear out: 'I have led you forty years in the wilderness: your clothes are not waxen old upon you, and thy shoe is not waxen old upon thy foot' (Deut. 29:5).

2. The miracle of the whole Syrian army smitten with blindness and then healed (2 Kings 6:15-20).

3. The miracle of the long day when the sun stood still (Josh. 10:12-13).

4. The miracle of the letter written by Elijah after he went to heaven (2 Chron. 21:12-15): one of the strangest supernatural events of the Bible. A study of the context reveals that the letter was written some time after Elijah was taken up. That had happened when Jehosophat was king; six years later Jehoram took the throne. He was a wicked king, whose wife was the daughter of the evil Queen Jezebel. Elijah's letter, warning him of the consequences of his wickedness, was written about eight years after the prophet was taken up into heaven!

5. The miracle of the dead soldier who was thrown into the sepulchre where the prophet Elisha was buried, and who 'revived and stood up on his feet' as his body touched Elisha's bones (2 Kings 13:21).

6. The miracle of the predicted day of Christ's death: 'from the going forth of the commandment to restore and to build Jerusalem unto the Messiah the Prince shall be seven weeks, and threescore and two weeks . . . and after threescore and two weeks shall Messiah be cut off' (Dan. 9:25-26). Threescore and two weeks plus seven weeks is 69 weeks. We know from Genesis 29:27 that a full week meant seven years, so 69 weeks means 483 years. So Daniel was saying that 483 years after the commandment to rebuild Jerusalem the Messiah shall come, and be 'cut off' – or die. Christ's death actually did occur approximately five centuries later.

7. The miracle of the conversion of Manasseh, one of the most wicked kings in the Bible. He had an appalling record of bloodshed and idolatory (2 Kings 21; 2 Chron. 33), yet when he besought the Lord God he was saved and became a transformed man (2 Chron. 33:11-16).

8. The miracle of Paul's transportation to heaven and back (2 Cor. 12:2-4).

9. The miracle of the prophecy of the 1335 days. Islam dates from 622 A.D., and came to be the dominant

religion in the whole of the Middle East, North Africa, and Spain. Israel was under Muslim domination for centuries. But in Daniel 12:12 it is prophesied, 'Blessed is he that waiteth, and cometh to the thousand three hundred and five and thirty days'. Days usually represent years in the Old Testament (Num. 14:34; Ezek. 4:6). The 1335th year according to the Islamic calendar, which dates from 622, is 1917, the year of the Balfour declaration, which pledged a national Jewish homeland. The modern state of Israel was born from this declaration – a fulfilment of a prophecy made thousands of years before in the Bible!

The Bible is truly a book of miracles, and I live by those miracles, and rely on the God of the supernatural. When I walked into that studio in Auckland my only reliance was on the God of miracle power. I thrive on miracles; my very life and breath depends on them!

In a ministry like mine with its daily problems and pressures: huge missions with their dense crowds and endless stream of sick and broken people; constant pressure from sensationalist media; the cost financially and in human terms of taking our missions all over the world; then miracles are the only answer. And I assure you that if God can perform miracles through me he can do it for anyone.

On a television interview recently I was asked what was the basis of my belief in miracles. I replied, 'I base my faith in miracles upon the life of Jesus Christ himself . . . he is the greatest single miracle of all time. His whole life and actions and love were a miracle.'

Jesus is a continuous miracle to the world. We cannot speak or think of miracles without looking at his whole life and being. He is the everlasting Redeemer, the very source and nourisher of our existence. The greatest discovery you can ever make is to know that we have a miraculous God. That is what this book is about: *the miracle that is Christ*!

2: The Miracle of Christ's Condescension

Edward Robertson wrote:

Ancient of days before the realm of time,
Eternal majesty of regions all sublime;
The mighty God, the all-creating Lord,
Resplendent King by angel hosts adored;
Effulgent Prince of life and light and love,
Supreme designer of all things above.
Sought earthly visitation.

Withdrawn from splendour regal and divine,
He who from untold ages did enshrine
The wisdom and the power of Godhead bright
Before he bore the rigours of the night;
Forsook sapphire throne and golden chalice,
Vacated royal court and iv'ry palace.
Sought human habitation.

And he whose ageless years shall know no end,
In answer to the cry: 'Whom shall I send?'
Resigned the jurisdiction of the stars,
Orion, Pallas, Mazzaroth and Mars;
Found new relationships of lowly plane,
Knew intimately sorrow, tears and pain.
Sought man's emancipation.

A while ago I was being interviewed on BBC Radio, and the interviewer was doing his best to try to catch me out. 'How do we know that Christianity is the right religion,' he asked, 'given that it isn't the oldest religion?'

I thought for a moment and then Jesus' words flashed into my mind: 'And now, O Father, glorify thou me with thine own self with the glory which I had with thee before the world was' (John 17:5). So I answered, 'Well, Jesus shared the glory with the Father before creation – you can't go back much further than that!' The interviewer was momentarily silenced. Then he replied meekly, 'Well, I guess you must be right, Mr Banks,' and moved on quickly to another question.

Christ always was and always is; he has no beginning or end; he is the alpha and omega. Here is the mystery of holiness, the mystery of divine liberality: 'He that spared not his own Son, but delivered him up for us all, how shall he not with him also freely give us all things?' (Rom. 8:32); 'though he was rich, yet for your sakes he became poor, that ye through his poverty might be rich' (2 Cor. 8:9).

How great was his condescension, to come down to this sin-cursed world, from heaven's glory to earth's poverty; from the adoration of angels to the rejection of humankind. David foresaw it hundreds of years before: 'Your gentleness and condescension have made me great' (Ps. 18:35 Amplified).

Imagine a sick child whose mother is away from home. The mother might send any number of beautiful and valuable gifts, but they would not help the child, who would yearn only for the comfort of its mother's presence. And, as a sick and troubled child needs a parent's personal presence, so a sick and troubled world needed the actual presence of its own creator. And in his great mercy, he came.

We can never understand what it cost him to come. Well may we sing:

> Oh, make me understand it,
>   Help me to take it in,
> What it cost you, God's Holy One,
>   To bear away my sin.

I remember when I was a small boy and, for the first time, heard King George VI speaking on the radio. It was Christmas day, and we were all huddled around the old wireless set in our little Wiltshire cottage, waiting with bated breath, until at last we heard: *'This is the King speaking to you.'* But the *King of Kings* has spoken to us; he visited this poor world of ours. The early Christians did not, like us, say, 'Look what the world has come to!'; instead they cried, *'Look what has come to the world!'*

George Duncan said, 'The Incarnation . . . is the miracle that lies at the heart of the Christian faith. Humanity is the only level of life man understands . . . if God wanted to reveal himself it is surely reasonable to expect that it would be on that human level that he would choose to do it.' Artists have used oils and marble to express the divine; poets have used the written word; and composers, music; but God chose to use living human flesh as the vehicle for expressing his own divine self.

Martin Luther wrote, 'Rejoice in the Incarnation. Trust that it occurred, even though apparently unreasonable and almost too wonderful . . . no longer are we aliens . . . under his wrath . . . Christ partook of our nature . . . the God-child fellowshipped with men, that they may have fellowship with God.'

God did not send a messenger to tell us about his love; he did not send a teacher to teach his love; he did

34

not send a lawyer to prove his love. He came himself, born to a human mother. And, as prophesied, he was called Emmanuel – God with us.

George Hudson of York, nicknamed 'the railway king' made a fortune in the early days of British railways. He was once able to use his influence to help a friend of the Duke of Wellington, and the Duke called to thank him and ask if there was any way he could return the favour. Hudson himself needed no favours, but he asked if there was anything the Duke could do for his daughter. She had been sent to an exclusive finishing school but she found that the other girls there, who came from aristocratic backgrounds, despised her because her father was a northern businessman.

A few days later the ducal carriage stopped outside the door of the academy, and the Duke of Wellington alighted, and asked for Miss Hudson. He took the girl by the arm and walked around the garden with her, chatting as to an intimate friend, while the other girls looked on in wonder and envy. No one could look down on Miss Hudson now. She was a friend of the greatest man in the land. His condescension had made her great. And that is just what Jesus has done for us!

When our blessed Lord stooped to visit earth in his Incarnation, he shared our human nature in order to redeem it. He humbled himself to death on the cross to atone for our sins. His humbling of himself lifts us to unimaginable heights. It has made us a special people: 'Ye are a chosen generation, a royal priesthood, a holy nation, a peculiar people; that ye should show forth the praises of him who hath called you out of darkness into his marvellous light' (1 Pet. 2:9).

The French philosopher Blaise Pascal said, 'The Incarnation shows man the greatness of his misery . . . by the greatness of the remedy which he required.'

There is a story of a little girl whose father had been away working for some time. One day he phoned his wife and she handed over the phone to the child, saying, 'Daddy wants to talk to you.' The little girl recognised her father's voice and began to cry. 'What's the matter?' asked her mother. The child looked despairingly at the mouthpiece of the telephone. 'It's Daddy,' she sobbed. 'How can we get him out of that hole?' God came to get us out of the hole we are in!

I was talking recently to one of Britain's finest pastors, minister of a large Midlands church. As we sat down for a hamburger at McDonalds after the huge meeting where we had preached, he said to me, 'My God, Melvin, this country is in a mess!' I could only agree: we are, and always have been, in a mess. But our hope is in the fact that God provided the Saviour to get us out of our mess. His promise, from Genesis to Malachi, is that he would send a Saviour to his undeserving people. And he kept that promise. He sent us Jesus to die for us, and he raised him from the dead. As C S Lewis put it, 'He paid us the intolerable compliment of loving us'.

Jesus came to this planet to save individual souls. He talked to the woman at the well; he touched the one blind man in the crowd; he wept for his friend Lazarus; took a child onto his knee. He talked of the one lost coin, the one lost sheep.

T E Lawrence, the famous Lawrence of Arabia, was travelling across the desert with a company of tribal Arabs, when a sandstorm blew up. One of the young Arab boys somehow got left behind and lost. Lawrence wanted to go back to find the boy, but the storm was becoming heavier, and the Arabs told Lawrence to keep his camel close to theirs. 'You never go back into a storm,' they told him. They could not understand Lawrence's concern – the lost Arab was, after all, only a boy, and a member of a low-status tribe as well. But Lawrence ignored their scoffing and warnings of danger and went back into the storm. Hours later he returned to the company, with the boy safely mounted on his camel. From that day the Arabs respected and admired Lawrence, because he had risked his own personal safety for the sake of one poor, lost boy. And in the same way Jesus cares for the soul of each individual person; he would have come down from heaven for just one lost soul.

Years ago the mayor of Boston decided that he wanted to see how the poorest people of his city lived. He let his beard grow, put on shabby clothes, and found lodgings for himself in a cheap boarding house in the slums. He was asked to chop wood to pay for his meagre breakfast. Never having done such work, the mayor was making a poor job of it but a young man took pity on him and did the work for him. The mayor then told the young man who he was, and asked him to report to his office that afternoon. The young man was rewarded with a good job but, although the mayor had asked him to tell no one about the circumstances of their meeting, he could not resist telling the story. Eventually a newspaper got hold of the story and ran the headline, 'THE GREATEST SOCIAL STOOP IN THE WORLD'. How well those words apply to the Incarnation! God stooped so low to bring salvation to the human race.

This incursion into our world of darkness and despair, sorrow and death, is the most amazing event that has ever happened. The Lord of glory came to earth, from out of the ivory palaces, his garments redolent with the fragrance of incense. But in order to live among us he had to lay all this glory aside. He had to take on human form. He who had dwelt with the Creator had to sink to the weakness of the created, nurture himself at a human mother's breast, and grow to man's stature, although he fills all things (Eph. 4:10). As the prophets foretold he came 'made of woman', the child of a virgin.

Jesus 'thought it not robbery to be equal with God, but made himself of no reputation, and took upon him the form of a servant, and was made in the likeness of men' (Phil. 2:6-7). He was and always will be equal to the Father. Though he took on human form, he is God himself, who humbled himself to come alongside us to help us in our needs, our sorrows, our guilt and sin.

Oh, the wonder of it! He lived in sinless glory where all power and all delights beyond our imaginings were his, but he left all this to take us by the hand. The Holy One of God took on all the trials and turmoils and frustrations of earthly existence. He carried our cause through the darkness of death and defeat and into the eternal area of everlasting triumph.

During the First World War in France, soldiers in the trenches saw one of their number fall in no-man's-land. He was still alive but badly wounded. A young private who was his closest friend told his officer that he would go and bring him back. The officer refused permission: he did not want the private to expose himself to such danger. But the young soldier disobeyed his officer and went out to his friend. As he staggered back to the trenches carrying his friend's body he was shot by machine gun fire and fell back into the trench, mortally wounded. The angry officer leaned over him. 'I told you not to go. Your friend is dead and now you are dying. I have lost two good men; it wasn't worth it!' With his dying breath the private replied, 'But it was worth it, sir, because when I got to him he said, "Jim, I knew you'd come".' God heard our cry and he came to us. He proved his faithfulness and love by giving his life for us. He kept his promise and came to save us.

Dora Greenwell wrote:

> He did not come to judge the world,
> He did not come to blame;
> He did not only come to seek,
> It was to save he came.
> And when we call him Saviour,
> Then we call him by his name.

He became identified with us, one with us, while possessing essential deity, co-partner with the Father. 'We beheld his glory, the glory as of the only begotten of the Father, full of grace and truth' (John 1:14). We saw the glory of the divine Son, his works, his words, his life. As John Wesley said, 'He never divested himself of his essential deity.' He did not lose his divinity by coming to earth. Rather he temporarily restricted himself and held a self-imposed limitation upon his divinity. Early theologians spoke of the *hypostatic union*, meaning that both divine and human nature blended together in the one person.

The Incarnation is a miracle and a mystery: the infinite became finite; the invisible became tangible. When Christ left heaven for us the world knew the double miracle of a virgin birth and a human being without sin.

The word *incarnation* comes from the Latin words meaning 'in' and 'flesh', and the doctrine is that at a given point in time God took upon himself human flesh and human nature. John 1:14 says, 'the Word was made flesh, and dwelt among us.' The Greek word translated as *dwelt* is connected with living in tents and suggests impermanence.

The Bible stresses the importance of the Incarnation: 'Every spirit that confesseth that Jesus is come in the flesh is of God, and every spirit that confesseth not that Jesus is come in the flesh is not of God, and this is that spirit of anti-Christ' (1 John 4:2-3).

The Incarnation Was A Perfect Union Of Two Natures

The Athanasian Creed calls Christ 'perfect God and perfect man'. And these two perfect natures of deity and humanity meet in perfect union. Pope Leo the Great said, '. . . two natures met together in one Redeemer. Nothing is wanting in either: entire majesty and entire humility. The same person is capable of death and the conquest of death. God knit himself to mankind in pity and in power.'

The two natures balance each other and make a complete whole. No one would go into a restaurant hungry and thirsty and order food without a drink or a drink but no food. Our bodies need both kinds of sustenance, and our souls respond to the two natures of God. Their union is represented symbolically in the offering of Leviticus 2, where the fine flour, representing human nature, was mixed with oil, representing the Holy Spirit. After being baked the offering was anointed with oil, symbolising the spirits of God and humanity united in Christ.

It Was A Purposeful Union

God delights to unfold himself; his purposes are ever developing and ever ripening. In the Incarnation we see the ultimate fulfilment of God's purposes.

When Christ emptied himself of the prerogatives of deity and came to this dark world to live, teach and heal, and to die on the cross, God was working out his divine purpose. For on the third day he rose again, for God had promised that evil would not triumph. He had promised that the woman's seed would bruise Satan (Gen. 3:15), and he sent his Son to conquer the works of the Evil One: 'For this purpose the Son of God was manifested, that he might destroy the works of the devil' (1 John 3:8); 'through death he might destroy him that had the power of death, that is, the devil' (Heb. 2:14).

When God wanted to save humanity he did not send a message or even an angel. He came himself. As Dr Brasnell Bonsall said, 'He became in Christ what we are, that we might become what he is. He became man that we might be raised to the central height of Godhead.'

It Was A Permanent Union

The humanity of our Lord was not something that he laid aside when he returned to heaven. He still remains a man, and will never cease to be one. When he became a man, it was for ever. There is a human being in the glory now!

God is a spirit, but he came to the earth as a man, and it was as a man he was born; as a man he taught, healed, and died. As a man he ascended and is able to plead for us in the glory. As a man he will come again to judge the world. 'There is one God and one mediator between God and men, *the man Christ Jesus*' (1 Tim. 2:5). He came to our world so that we might, one day, be able to go to his. In the Incarnation we see deity on the streets of the world; in the Resurrection and Ascension we see humanity on the streets of heaven!

Christ's coming brought light and hope to a world of darkness. The arms of Oxford University is an open book with the Latin words *Dominus illuminatio mea*: the Lord is my light.

'Before the mountains were brought forth, or ever thou hadst formed the earth and the world, even from everlasting to everlasting, thou art God' (Ps. 90:2). It is wonderful to think that this was the God who came down to earth for us. Charles Wesley expressed it as, 'God incomprehensibly made man.'

Jesus came to do his Father's will on our earth; his will became earth-bound, earth-expressed; earth-channelled. For this dark, hard world, for men and women crushed and defeated, he made the journey to reach us. Francis Thompson speaks of the hope this gives us:

But (when so sad thou canst not sadder)
    Cry – and upon thy so sore loss
Shall shine the traffic of Jacob's ladder
    Pitched between heaven and Charing Cross.

Yea, in the night, my Soul, my daughter,
    Cry – clinging Heaven by the hems;
And lo, Christ walking on the water,
    Not of Gennesareth, but Thames!

Just before he died, the great theologian Karl Barth was asked what was his hope for the world. He replied, 'That there would be a gradual revelation of the purpose for Christ's coming into the world, in that he reconciled us to God. This is my great hope.' *May we understand the great miracle of Christ's condescension, the foundation to all his miracles, the first step to the greatest miracle of all.*

3: The Miracle of Christ's Holiness

Holiness is godliness with guts, with courage, with backbone behind it.

Eric Delve

The character of Jesus is, in itself, an astounding miracle. There is perfection in his nature, in his works, in every aspect of his person. Tennyson said of him, 'His character was more wonderful than his miracles.' But the fact is that his miracles were a result of his character. Even his enemies acknowledged his perfection: Pilate said, 'I find no fault with this man.'

Jesus walked through this sinful world yet remained spotless. Where the first Adam failed, the second Adam triumphed. The devil tried him with every temptation, yet still Christ resisted and remained without sin. Peter, in a reference to the messianic prophesy of Isaiah, said of Jesus, 'He committed no sin, and no deceit was found in his mouth' (1 Pet. 2:22).

The greatest need for the believer is to become like Jesus, to be changed and made new by the Holy Spirit, and take on the character of Jesus. John says that we cannot claim to live in Christ if we do not walk as he walked (1 John 2:6). This is what holiness means.

God wants his children to be holy. Holiness, or sanctification, is connected in the Scriptures with ideas of dedication and cleansing. God wants us to be cleansed from evil and selfishness and dedicated to his will, filled with his love and power. He wants us to yield ourselves to the process of the Holy Spirit, whose work of dedication and sanctification produces inner peace in our lives, ends frustration, lifts burdens and doubts, frees us from striving and selfish personal ambition.

We cannot be holy, cannot be like Jesus, unless we *know* his character. St Augustine said, 'Who can call on thee, not knowing thee?' Spurgeon wrote, 'the highest science which can engage the attention of the child of God is the name, the nature, the person, the works, the doings . . . of the great God.' Paul said, 'I count all things but loss for the excellency of *the knowledge of Christ Jesus my Lord.*'

It is wonderful, elevating, and joyful to know the character of Jesus and for that to become our own character. As a boy I remember singing at Salvation Army meetings:

> Let the beauty of Jesus be seen in me,
> All his wonderful power and purity.

God is the creator of harmony, beauty, and truth, and can be satisfied with nothing less: 'As he which has called you is holy, so be ye holy' (1 Pet. 1:15).

Our thoughts, behaviour, standards, and whole lifestyle as Christians are a response to the character of Christ. It inspires, and is the basis for, our faith and trust in him. But it is impossible to trust someone one does not know. Our Christian life depends on our understanding fully who Jesus is. We can only become like him, become holy, if we know him and understand what he desires for us. God is perfect in all his works and he created us in his image, wanting us to share the perfection of his nature. Holiness is not an optional extra, but an essential for Christians.

A couple of years ago I visited the Outer Hebrides off the west coast of Scotland, the scene of an amazing revival in the early 1950s, when people were weeping with contrition openly on the streets, churches remained open all night, whole communities were struck by the power of God. Thousands were converted to Christ. I wanted to find out what was at the root of this divine visitation and was told that the key was 'a spirit of exceeding deep humility, *holiness*, love, and persistence in intercession.' Duncan Campbell, who was so greatly used in that revival, wrote, 'a baptism of holiness, a demonstration of godly living, is the crying need of our day.'

I want to share with you ten scriptural reasons why we should seek to share the holy character of Christ.

1. God Wants Us To Be Holy

'This is the will of God, even our sanctification' (1 Thess. 4:3). It is no good repeating the Lord's prayer, and saying, 'Thy will be done' if, knowing God's will, we do not obey it. What God requires from us is for our good and our happiness. He is all-knowing, wise, and loving, and desires us to embrace his good, acceptable, and perfect will.

2. God Commands Us To Be Holy

Jesus gives a very clear command in Matthew 5:48: 'Be ye therefore perfect, even as your Father which is in heaven is perfect'. This sounds to many of us like a daunting command, but we can be perfect in that we can be perfectly cleansed from sin; we can be perfectly yielded to God's will; we can be perfectly attuned to his voice, guided by it and walking in his way day by day.

We cannot have absolute sinlessness or absolute perfection but we can have before us the perfection of God's character as our ultimate goal and ideal. We can have the joy of letting his Spirit and character form in us, and manifesting his holiness in our daily conduct. Paul admits that he is not yet perfect: 'Not as though I had already attained, either were already perfect . . . but . . . I press toward the mark' (Phil.3:12-14). Yet later, in verse 15 he says, 'Let us therefore, as many as be perfect, be thus minded . . .'. So despite his realisation of his own human failings, there is a sense in which Paul can claim perfection. He is perfectly forgiven and cleansed, perfectly yielded to God's will for his life, and perfectly filled with the Holy Spirit. God urges us to seek perfect cleansing: 'And every man that hath this hope in him purifieth himself, even as he is pure.'

3. God's Prayer Is That We Should Be Holy

Jesus prays for the sanctification of his disciples in John 17:17: 'Sanctify them through thy truth', and goes on to pray not just for his present disciples but for those who would believe in later years: '. . . that they also might be sanctified . . . neither pray I for these alone, but for them also which shall believe on me through their word' (John 17:19-20). That means you and me!

If the Lord prayed then that we should be sanctified and be like him, I believe that is what he is still praying for us today. I am sure he is praying daily for each one of his children that we should know the joy of seeing his character miraculously forming in us. 'He is able to save

46

them to the uttermost that come unto God by him, seeing *he ever liveth to make intercession for them*' (Heb. 7:25).

In the *Arabian Nights* story, Aladdin acquires a lamp which turns out to have magic powers. Whenever he rubs it a genie appears, and he need only express a wish for the genie to grant it. Soon Aladdin has everything he desires: all his needs are met and all his problems solved by means of the magic lamp. Sometimes we want God to answer our prayers like that, but that is not the way he works. His intercession for us is continuous but he desires us to establish a stable, daily fellowship with him – not to seek instant answers to prayer only when we are in particular trouble. It is sometimes hard for us to comprehend that God cares about our daily needs. Someone who was told this by a friend protested, 'But God is so busy.' 'Yes,' the friend replied, 'but his business is you!'

4. God Promises Us Holiness

St Augustine prayed, 'Command what thou wilt, but give what thou commandest.' When God reveals his will for us, or gives us a command, he always gives us the power to obey it. An old Scottish lady used to say, 'All God's biddings are enablings.' A loving, kind, and all-wise God does not command us to seek something which is impossible for us. If he commands us to be holy, then he will give us the power to be so.

When William Booth lay dying he was heard to say, 'The promises of God are sure, if you only believe.' God has promised to give us his character, to make us holy, if we believe and claim his promises. 'The very God of peace sanctify you wholly . . . faithful is he that calleth you, *who also will do it*' (1 Thess. 5:23-24). Paul says that Abraham, 'was strong in faith, giving glory to God; and being fully persuaded that *what he had promised, he was able also to perform*' (Rom. 4:20-21).

Let us hold fast to this promise of God. We often sing in our meetings:

> We are building a people of power,
> We are building a people of praise.

Let us not forget that we are also building *a people of purity!* Paul exorts us, 'Having therefore these promises . . . let us cleanse ourselves from all filthiness of the flesh and spirit, perfecting holiness in the fear of God' (2 Cor. 7:1).

There are said to be 30,000 promises in the Bible. Thank God that he keeps his promises! 'God is not a man that he should lie' (Num.23:19). Let us believe the promises of God, hold fast and embrace them, and enter into a holy experience with our maker. Isaac Watts wrote, 'I believe the promises of God enough to venture out on eternity on them.' *Stake your claim daily on God's promise to make you holy.*

5. God Wants Us To Be Fruitful In Outreach Through Holiness

Look at Peter in Luke 22:55-60. He did not have the courage to witness to his faith even before individuals. But when he had been filled and sanctified by the Holy Ghost he was endued with such power that he won 3,000 souls in one day! Jesus said, 'Ye shall receive power, after that the Holy Ghost has come upon you: and ye shall be witnesses unto me . . .' (Acts 1:8). We have little power to make an impact in outreach unless we are empowered by God's Holy Spirit.

People have so often asked me to 'pray for my husband to come to Christ', or 'pray for my wife to believe'. I tell these people, 'Show them love, love cannot be resisted; live as if Jesus was in the home.' In other words: have the character of God, show the spirit of Jesus.

Years ago a Christian businessman was expecting the famous Cliff College principal Thomas Cook to come to preach at his local chapel and stay at his home. He was very anxious to have everything just right and kept issuing orders to the maid to do this and do that until she grew tired of hearing about Thomas Cook. When she went off shopping to buy the meat for the great man she started gossiping to the butcher. 'All I hear is Thomas Cook! Thomas Cook . . . do this, Thomas Cook . . . do that, you'd think Jesus Christ was coming to lunch!'

On Sunday Thomas Cook arrived. The maid was struck by his kindness and consideration to her, and the way he took an interest in her. She became captivated by the godliness of his character. They talked together and he led her to Christ. She was radiant with joy and peace. The next day she went off to buy meat and the butcher asked her jokingly, 'How did it go yesterday? Did Jesus Christ come to lunch?' She quietly replied, 'I believe he did.'

That woman was won to Christ because the character of Jesus was in Thomas Cook. He was holy as our Lord was holy. Our prayers for the lost have new power as we are transformed in our personal lives by the Holy Spirit. A man was once telling another about his Lord. His face shone with joy, his eyes sparkled with light, his whole appearance reflected the radiance and tranquility of his personality. The unsaved man replied to the gospel challenge with the words, 'I can *see* what you're saying!'

We see such evils in our society. So much greed,

selfishness, and sin – such a denial of light. It is the miraculous character of Jesus that brings light into a world of darkness. We cannot hope for a revival if we are not a holy people. In the early 1950s hundreds of churches in London were planning a crusade. They had all that was necessary in terms of money, organisation, and human effort – but revival did not come. God was bringing revival at that time, but he was working with no organisation, no huge battalions to back him, just two holy old ladies in the Outer Hebrides! Through those two godly women a great revival broke out in those tiny scattered islands. It was through the missionaries who humbly confessed their sins and sought God's purity that revival came to Ruanda, bringing tens of thousands of true converts to Christ. It was the zealous and devoted disciples in Korea, who were seeking holiness in fasting and prayer, that God visited, with the result of the eventual establishment of the largest church in the world. When the godly but then little-known evangelist Tommy Hicks lay sick and dying, God raised him up, later sending him to the Argentine where he was the instrument of God's working a mighty revival where 500,000 came to Christ.

Holiness and successful soul-winning are inseparable. If we pray for revival we must first pray for our own holiness.

6. God Gave Us An Example Of Holiness In Christ

The life of Jesus exemplifies pure, sanctified, holy living. 'And for their sakes I sanctify myself, that they also might be sanctified by the truth' (John 17:19). In his own life Jesus provided the perfect illustration of all he taught about godly living. And it is by seeing the beauty of his pure life and character that we are brought to conviction about our own sin and need. Isaiah was sanctified by a vision of the holiness of the Lord (Isa. 6). Though his reaction to seeing such holiness was a consciousness of his own unclean nature, the Lord cleansed him and took away his sin.

We must not be discouraged by our own unworthiness. We should look, not at our own weakness, but at God's power. So many in the Bible were daunted by their own unworthiness: Moses thought he was inadequate, Gideon thought he was too poor and obscure, Jeremiah thought he was too young. Remember David's despair, Peter's backsliding, Thomas's doubting. But to all these and millions of others through the centuries God proved that 'the word of God is not bound' (2 Tim. 2:9). The victories they gained, the fulfilled lives they led, proved that God could turn failure into success. Confronted with your need, your problems, your shortcomings, he can make you 'more than conquerors'.

Jesus set the example of holiness. When he comes into our lives the Holy One of God has come to dwell in us and we can have the mind of God, see things with his eyes, and take on his characteristics. It was said of St Francis of Assisi, 'He sees the way God sees.' As we contemplate daily the nature of our Lord, his holiness becomes our holiness and his character our character.

7. God's Son Died To Make Us Holy

Paul tells us that Christ died to make his church pure and holy: 'Christ loved the church and gave himself for it; that he might sanctify and cleanse it . . . that he might present it to himself a glorious church . . . holy and without blemish' (Eph. 5:25-27). In Hebrews we are reminded that 'we are sanctified through the offering of the body of Jesus Christ' and 'he hath perfected forever they that are sanctified' (Heb. 10:10,14).

'The blood of Jesus Christ . . . cleanseth us from all sin' (1 John 1:7). I remember as a teenager marching behind the colours of the Salvation Army. The words that William Booth put on the flag became emblazoned on my mind – *blood and fire* – with their message of Calvary's blood and the purifying power of the Holy Spirit.

Jesus took all our unholiness upon him when he suffered on the cross: 'he hath borne our griefs and carried our sorrows . . . he was wounded for our transgressions, he was bruised for our iniquities' (Isa. 53:4-5). He suffered so that we might be able to be holy. Colin Urquhart said, 'Trying to be holy in your own strength is like trying to swim the Atlantic, but allowing the Holy Spirit to operate in your life, and work his holy ministry through you, is like being carried across the Atlantic by plane.' If we desire holiness of character we must kneel in humility and obedience at the wounded feet of the crucified, living Christ.

8. God Wants Us To Be Holy For The Lord's Return

If you were summoned to meet the Queen you would not appear with a dirty face and greasy hair. You would probably take days to prepare yourself and arrive clean, well-groomed, and dressed in your best. Even Bob Geldof had a shave and put on a suit to collect his knighthood! So should we not, as the Lord's return nears, prepare ourselves to be pure and clean, ready to meet the King of kings?

Years ago a rich man died in the United States. The minister at the funeral was talking afterwards to one of his servants, an old black man. 'Well, Sam, I guess your good master is now in heaven.' The old man replied, 'Now, that's a hard question . . . I don't think he can be.' The minister was shocked and asked him why he said that. 'Well you see, sir,' explained Sam, 'my master was always very particular if he was going anywhere. If he was going off on holiday or on business he would always prepare days before. I always knew about it and he would give me plenty of time to get ready for it. But I never heard him talking about going to heaven. No, sir, I never did hear him say he was planning to go there!'

Have you made your preparations? We shall be looking again at the second coming later but it is important to note that, in the New Testament, references to this event are often linked with a call to holiness. Paul says, 'The very God of peace sanctify you wholly; and I pray God your whole spirit and soul and body be preserved blameless unto the coming of our Lord Jesus Christ' (1 Thess. 5:23). And Peter reminds us, 'But the day of the Lord will come . . . seeing then that all these things shall be dissolved, what manner of persons ought ye to be in all holy conversation and godliness' (2 Pet. 3:10,11).

We can never be wholly faultless in this life, but we can be blameless. A cup may be cheap and flawed but at least it can be clean! Jesus warns us to, 'watch . . . and pray always, that ye may be accounted worthy to escape all these things that shall come to pass' (Luke 21:36). We need to be holy as Jesus is holy, and 'so much more as ye see the day approaching' (Heb. 10:25).

9. God Needs Us To Be Holy For Heaven

There can be no sin in heaven: 'And there shall in no wise enter into it any thing that defileth' (Rev.21:27). No impurity, no hatred, no bitterness, no jealousy, no pride, can be tolerated in heaven. *It is a holy place for a holy people.*

Satan was once an angel of light but he was cast out of heaven when pride entered his heart (Isa. 14:12-15). Paul tells us to 'follow peace with all men, and holiness, without which no man shall see the Lord' (Heb. 12:14). Jesus said, 'Blessed are the pure in heart: for they shall see God' (Matt. 5:8). Our hope of glory is Christ in us: the thoughts, the motives, the love, the spirit of Jesus filling us. John says:

> Behold what manner of love the Father hath bestowed upon us, that we should be called the sons of God . . . now are we the sons of God, and it doth not yet appear what we shall be, but we know that, when he shall appear, we shall be like him; for we shall see him as he is. And every man who has this hope in him purifieth himself, even as he is pure. (1 John 3:1-3).

The American statesman Daniel Webster was always in trouble as a schoolboy. There is a story of him coming to school one day with filthy hands, just when the headmaster decided to inspect all the boys' hands. As the headmaster passed down the line, Webster just had time to lick one hand and wipe it on his shirt and this was the hand he held out for inspection. The headmaster took one look and said, 'Unless I find one hand dirtier than that in the school today I shall cane you.' Immediately Webster shot out his other, even filthier hand. The disconcerted headmaster had to keep his word, and

Webster escaped a caning! But there will be no excuses for our uncleanliness when the judgement comes. It says in Revelation: 'He which is filthy, let him be filthy still' (Rev.22:11).

10. God Shows Us How Christ's Holiness Can Be Seen In Our Lives

The marks of holiness in a Christian's character are clearly seen. Those who are like Jesus think constantly about him; they love to read, hear, and talk about him; they are jealous for his name and honour; they delight to please him; they long to be with him always.

We must seek the anointed life, the spotless life, the impeccable and beautiful life of Jesus. He is beauty beyond beauty, wonder beyond wonder, marvel beyond marvel. And he offers his own amazing character to us, who are so undeserving, so unclean, so weak and sinful. *That is the miracle of Christ's character!*

4: The Miracle of Christ's Claims

'*I see the way*' – Confucius
'*I can show you the way*' – Krishna
'*I am seeking the way*' – Buddha
but Jesus said – '*I am the way*'

I was prayerfully preparing my message before a service in the south of England when the minister who was organising the mission entered. He had with him a reporter and photographer from the local press. I was not surprised as this is normal practice when we hold missions in English towns, but I was somewhat taken aback when the reporter, with no preliminary courtesies, fired straight at me, 'This is certainly some claim you're making that miracles happen in these services, Rev. Banks!' I looked up from my Bible, showed him the book, and quietly responded, 'The works that I do ye shall do also.' That night God's great power was demonstrated in miraculous events, and the reporter was convinced of the claims of Christ.

Jesus was the greatest man who ever lived and he made the greatest claims – astonishing claims. They are profound, far-reaching, amazing claims; yet they are also simple, realistic, and practical. In some English churches where I preach the people seem to think that a good preacher is an incomprehensible one. If they can understand what's being said then it can't be good stuff! Yet Jesus' claims were simple enough and clear enough for anyone to understand: 'the wayfaring men, though fools, shall not err therein' (Isa. 35:8).

Jesus Claimed That God Was His Father

When Jesus healed the man who had been an invalid for 38 years (John 5) he was accused of sabbath-breaking and, in rebutting this charge, made some startling claims for himself. He began by referring to God as *'my Father'*. Some modern theologians try to diminish the great significance of these words. But the contemporaries of Jesus knew just how momentous they were: they 'sought the more to kill him, because he had not only broken the sabbath, but said also that God was his Father, making himself equal with God (John 5:18). And when Jesus was accused before Pilate his enemies said, 'by our law he ought to die because he made himself the Son of God' (John 19:7).

Jesus certainly intended his claim to a unique relationship with God to be understood in this way, and he emphasised it by frequent references to himself as 'the Son'. There is no doubt that Jesus claimed divinity and, although he encourages us to think of God intimately, as a father, he makes a distinction between his relationship with God and ours. He taught his disciples to pray 'Our Father' and spoke to them of God as 'your Father', but he himself addressed God as 'my Father'. The message that the Risen Christ gave Mary to take to his disciples was, 'I ascend unto my Father, and your Father; and to my God, and your God'(John 20:17) – not 'our Father' and 'our God'.

Jesus claimed that he and the Father are so closely identified as to be One (John 10:30) and that to receive him is to receive God (Matt. 10:40). To despise Jesus is to despise God (Luke 10:16) and to see Jesus is to see God (John 14:9). And when the resurrected Christ accepts worship from the apostle Thomas, who exclaimed 'my Lord and my God' (John 20:28), he was implicitly claiming deity.

He Claimed That He Does God's Works

Because he is God Jesus claims to do the works of God: 'I must work the works of him who sent me' (John 9:4). The works of a supernatural God are miraculous, so miracles have to be one of Christ's credentials. When John the Baptist in prison sent messengers to Jesus to ask if he was 'he that should come' Jesus replied, 'Tell John what things ye have seen and heard; how that the blind see, the lame walk, the lepers are cleansed, the deaf hear, the dead are raised' (Luke 7:21). Jesus was claiming by this response that his miracles proved him to be the Messiah. Others may have been claiming miracles at that time, but true miracles are not conjuring tricks. Jesus refused to work miracles to satisfy the curiosity of the Scribes and Pharisees (Matt. 12:38-39), to entertain Herod (Luke 23:8-9), or in response to Satan's temptation (Matt. 4:1-10).

Jesus' miracles displayed the authority of God: 'And they were all amazed . . . saying, what thing is this? . . . for with authority commandeth he even the unclean spirits, and they do obey him' (Mark 1:27). Most importantly, *Jesus' miracles glorified God*: 'When the multitudes saw it [the healing of a palsied man] they marvelled and glorified God' (Matt. 9:8). And when Jesus raised the widow of Nain's son the people 'glorified God, saying . . . that God hath visited his people' (Luke 7:16).

The prominence given to Christ's miracles in the

Gospel narratives shows their importance. Jesus himself advanced the argument that his miracles were proof enough of his claims (John 10:38). The miracles of Jesus are not presented in Scripture as optional extras appended to the gospel, but as the natural result of God's presence – as natural as the fruiting of an apple tree. When God is present his power and authority are manifest.

When Jesus speaks of the works of God he is not only referring to miracles. He includes also the preaching of the gospel to the poor (Luke 7:22) and the forgiveness of sins. One miracle was worked just to make this point. When the sick man was lowered through the roof by his friends (Mark 2), Jesus said to him, 'Son, thy sins be forgiven thee.' This shocked some of the bystanders who thought it was blasphemous to offer forgiveness, which only God could give. Jesus knew their thoughts and asked 'Whether it is easier to say to the sick . . . Thy sins be forgiven thee, or to say, Arise and take up your bed and walk?' He was implying that the former was easier in that forgiveness is not outwardly manifested, but if Jesus claims healing for the man and he is not healed, then he is exposed as an imposter. And he goes on to heal the man, 'that ye may know that the Son of man hath power on earth to forgive sins.' His point is that whether in healing or the forgiveness of sins, his authority would produce results. The two aspects of God's authority in Christ are inextricably interwoven and to deny one is to deny the other.

Because only the divine Jesus, who has the authority of God, can forgive sins *he is the only way to salvation.* Jesus said, 'I am the way, the truth and the life: no man cometh unto the Father but by me' (John 14:6). Many religious leaders have claimed, 'I seek the way', 'I see the way', 'I know the way', 'I can show the way', but only Jesus Christ, the Son of God, has said *'I am the way'.*

In Gloucester, a city with a large Muslim community, I preached that Christ was the only way of salvation, and no other religion was needed. This was front page news and I was actually threatened with prosecution. I publicly declared my willingness to be the first man in England since Bunyan to be imprisoned for the gospel's sake. I was interviewed on television and radio where I pointed out that in 32 years of preaching the gospel I had never before been threatened with prosecution in Britain. Letters and telephone calls flooded newspaper offices and my own crusade office; three to one were supportive of my statement in Gloucester. When I returned to that city I was not arrested but allowed to hold a meeting where I repeated my statement that Jesus only is the way and the truth. One hundred people made a decision for Christ that day as a result.

The legendary schoolboy howler describes Jesus as 'God's only forgotten son' and indeed, his miraculous nature and claims are often forgotten today. There is a story of a minister's little daughter who went into her father's study when he was preparing a sermon. 'Does Jesus tell you what to say in your sermon?' she asked. 'Yes, dear.' 'Do you tell the people everything he tells you to say, Daddy?' 'Of course, dear,' her father replied. 'Then why have you crossed so much out?' Many ministers and many churches today have crossed out some of the most wonderful and miraculous of Christ's claims. But those claims and promises are as valid today as they ever were.

Jesus Claimed He Was The Resurrection And The Life

Jesus claimed the authority to raise the dead: 'For as the Father raiseth up the dead, and quickeneth them, even so the Son quickeneth whom he will . . . marvel not at this for the hour is coming, in the which all that are in the graves shall hear his voice' (John 5:21,28). This remarkable claim is given credence by the incidents of actual raising of the dead during Jesus' earthly ministry: Jairus's daughter, the widow's son, Lazarus.

Jesus proved that even death could not thwart his plans. After his Resurrection he actually kept an appointment that he had made before his death. He had told the disciples, 'after that I am risen, I will go before you into Galilee' (Mark 14:28). Outside the empty tomb they were reminded of this promise by the angel: 'He is risen . . . tell his disciples and Peter that he goeth before you into Galilee: there shall you see him, *as he said unto you*' (Mark 16:6-7). When Jesus says something he means it; when he makes a promise he keeps it. And he promises that he will raise the dead: every one of us, king and pauper, you and me.

Jesus will not only raise the dead but he will judge them: 'the Father . . . hath committed all judgment unto the Son . . . and hath given him authority to execute judgment also because he is the Son of man' (John 5:22,27). As the Son of man he is qualified to judge us because his Incarnation identified him with all the trials and temptations that beset the human race. He continues, 'as I hear, I judge, and my judgment is just' (John 5:30). He presents himself in the role of judge in explaining the parable of the tares to his disciples: 'The Son of man shall send forth his angels, and they shall gather out of his kingdom all things that offend, and them which do iniquity, and shall cast them into a furnace of fire' (Matt. 13:41-42). And in the parable of the sheep and goats he reveals that his criterion for judgment will be the attitude people had towards him, as manifested in their treatment of others. The Son of man comes in his glory and separates the sheep from the goats. The sheep, who inherit God's kingdom, are those who have fed the hungry, clothed the naked, visited the sick and imprisoned, for the Lord says, 'Inasmuch as ye have done it unto one of the least of these my brethren, ye have done it unto me.' The rejected goats are those who failed to feed the hungry, clothe the naked, visit the sick and imprisoned, for in neglecting these things they neglected the commands and example of the Lord (Matt. 25:31-46). That is, to take and live in Him.

Jesus Claimed Scriptural Testimony

In defending himself before his accusers Jesus said, 'Search the scriptures; for in them ye think ye have eternal life, and they are they which testify of me', and emphasises this scriptural testimony by claiming, 'Had you believed Moses ye would have believed me, for he wrote of me' (John 5:39,46). At the beginning of his public ministry he made the same assertion when he read from Isaiah, 'The spirit of the Lord is upon me, because he hath anointed me to preach the gospel to the poor . . .', and went on to say, 'This day is this scripture fulfilled in your ears' (Luke 4:17-21).

Jesus constantly described himself as having been 'sent' by his Father – a claim no ordinary mortal could make. Although he upholds the authority of Scripture he sometimes claims to have greater authority, as when he says, 'the Son of man is Lord also of the sabbath' (Mark 2:28), or 'in this place is one greater than the temple' (Matt. 12:6). In these statements Jesus is claiming authority equal to that of God.

Jesus Claims To Satisfy Our Deepest Needs

When I was on a crusade in a Muslim country a couple of years ago I read in their national newspaper on

Muhammad's birthday this comment from a leading Muslim theologian: 'Muhammad did not claim to be God or that he could do what only God can do'. But Jesus did make such claims! He claimed not only to be God and to do his works, but that he could do what only God can do: meet and satisfy the deepest needs of the human heart.

Jesus said, 'If any man thirst, let him come unto me and drink' (John 7:37). Some years ago I said on a television programme that if anyone wrote to me declaring truthfully that they had faithfully followed Christ's teachings but gained no peace, joy, or satisfaction, I would pay that person £1000. If only a few of the million viewers had taken me up I would have been bankrupt, for I did not have that sort of money! But I did not receive a single claim, though hundreds wrote to ask more about the way of peace and satisfaction through Christ. I was not surprised at this result for I know that Christ cannot lie, and only he can satisfy our hearts.

Jesus claimed that 'He that heareth my word, and believeth on him that sent me, hath everlasting life, and shall not come into condemnation, but is passed from death into life' (John 5:24). Look at the great 'I am' passages of John's Gospel: 'I am the bread of life' (6:35); 'I am the light of the world' (8:12); 'I am the door' (8:7); 'I am the resurrection and the life' (11:25); 'I am the way, the truth, and the life' (14:6); 'I am the true vine' (15:1). This term *I am* is an emphatic one, associated with the name of God and demonstrated in God's commission to Moses to deliver the children of Israel from bondage. Moses wanted to know how to answer the people when they asked on what authority he acted. 'And God said unto Moses, I AM THAT I AM: and he said, Thus shalt thou say unto the children of Israel,

I AM hath sent me unto you' (Ex. 3:14). Not 'I was' or 'I will be' but 'I am', the eternal and unchanging one whose title Jesus claimed as his own.

He who delivered Israel from bondage in Egypt can deliver souls from the bondage of sin. Jesus said, 'Come unto me, all ye that labour and are heavy laden, and I will give you rest' (Matt. 11:28). Only a charlatan or imposter could make this promise if he knew he was incapable of satisfying our hopes and aspirations. And Jesus is no imposter; what he promises he delivers.

In our crusades our aim is to bring to people the real Christ, the Christ who has been obscured by theology, religious traditions, and church structures. We want people to know the real Jesus who can free them from sin, doubt, and fear, the Jesus who can meet the needs of their hearts.

Jesus Claimed To Be The Messiah

Christ, from the Greek *Christos*, means 'anointed' and is the equivalent of the Hebrew word *Messiah*. The Jews anointed the occupants of three offices: prophets, priests, kings. No one could hold all three positions: David was both king and prophet but not priest; Jeremiah was priest and prophet but not king. Only Jesus Christ has occupied all three positions. His anointing came when the Holy Ghost descended upon him when he arose from the waters of baptism.

Jesus did not stress the Messiah aspect of his mission, probably because of the political overtones that the Jews associated with the title. They expected the Messiah to deliver them from the oppression of Roman rule and establish a world-wide empire, the very thing the devil tempted Jesus to do. Jesus told Pilate, 'My kingdom is not of this world' (John 18:36). However Jesus did accept the titles of Messiah and Christ. The Samaritan woman at the well 'saith unto him, I know that Messiah cometh, which is called Christ . . . Jesus saith unto her, I that speak unto thee am he' (John 4:25-26). When Peter declared, 'thou art the Christ, the Son of the living God', Jesus answered, '. . . flesh and blood hath not revealed it unto thee, but my Father which is in heaven' (Matt. 16:16-17). Jesus told the disciples not to reveal that he was the Christ, and 'from that time forth began Jesus to show unto his disciples how that he must go unto Jerusalem, and suffer many things . . . and be killed, and be raised again the third day' (Matt.16:21). Messiahship was not the path of fame and worldly power but the lowly path to the cross, to bring salvation to his people.

By claiming to be the Christ Jesus demands acceptance as the anointed prophet of God – the only true and complete revelation of God. 'God, who at sundry times and in diverse manners spake in time past unto the fathers by the prophets, hath in these last days spoken unto us by his Son' (Heb. 1:1-2).

Christ is also the anointed priest, who sacrificed himself on the altar of his cross and purged our sins. 'Neither is there salvation in any other, for there is none other name under heaven given among men, whereby we must be saved' (Acts 4:12).

Christ is also the anointed king demanding allegiance and obedience from his subjects: 'and the Lamb shall overcome them : for he is Lord of Lords, and King of kings' (Rev. 17:14). It is not acceptable to give Jesus less esteem than his status demands. Describing Jesus as a great teacher, a moral leader, a religious genius, or godly man, is to miss the point. There may be a connection here with the puzzling account of Jesus needing to pray twice for a blind man before he was completely cured (Mark 8:22-25). Was Jesus deliberately withholding complete healing the first time so as to make a point? Remember that the Bible is inspired by the Holy Spirit and events are not recorded in a random manner, but have structure and purpose. When Jesus first prayed for the blind man he received partial vision; when he prayed again his sight was fully restored. This incident is followed immediately by Jesus asking his disciples 'Whom do men say that I am?' They answered, 'John the Baptist, but some say Elias, and others one of the prophets'. These were all worthy titles but they revealed only a blurred and partial insight as to who Jesus was. He pressed, 'But whom say ye that I am?' and that is when Peter says, 'Thou art the Christ' (Mark 8:27-29). This was the revelation of full vision, and anything less is not enough.

The claims of Christ are clear and momentous and cannot be ignored. They demand a response from us. C S Lewis has pointed out, in *Mere Christianity*, that there are three options open to us in considering who Jesus is. Anyone making the claims that Jesus made has to be a deluded madman, a wicked imposter, or God himself. There is nothing in Jesus' words, life, or actions to make us doubt his sanity. If he were an imposter what would he gain from his deception? He gained no profit from his claims, but endured the cross for them, hardly the action of an imposter, who would have tried to save himself by recanting. Could a cheat and liar have exerted such a beneficial influence on society, turning sinners into saints? Jesus can only be God. His claims have been vindicated by people of all times and all races who testify to finding peace, healing, and salvation through him. He is all he claims to be and all that has been claimed for him in the Scriptures: the Messiah, the Prince of peace, our great high priest, our shepherd, the King of kings, God's own Son.

5: The Miracle of Christ's Words

Lord and Saviour, true and kind, Be the master of my mind.
An ancient prayer

What a gift to the world are words, conversation, writings! I am happiest when I can relax in bed, at home in my sun-lounge or garden, or on the rich grass of the beautiful Salisbury Plain, accompanied by a good book. I love to read, like Paul who asked Timothy to make sure he brought him 'the books, but especially the parchments' (2 Tim. 4:13). Spurgeon commented on this in the verse:

> He is inspired – yet he wants books!
> He has been preaching for 30 years – yet he wants books!
> He has a vast experience – yet he wants books!
> He has been caught up in the third heaven – yet he wants books!
> He has written the major part of the New Testament – yet he wants books!

Oswald Chambers, a man renowned for the holiness of his character wrote, 'my books are silent, healthy, loyal lovers . . . I thank God for books.' A politician who was an avid reader answered friends who asked how he had time to read, 'I don't have time – I take it!'

I love to read the works of writers who are masters of words: Shakespeare, Milton, Tennyson; and to read the great theologians of the past: Luther, Calvin, Zwingli. I love to listen to old records of preachers and speakers who were masters of communication: Peter Marshall, William Booth, Winston Churchill, Martin Luther King. But the greatest words ever spoken fell from the lips of the Master, he of whom it was said, 'Never spake a man like this man' (John 7:46).

The centurion who came to Jesus said, 'speak the word only, and my servant shall be healed' (Matt. 8:8). Jesus said, 'He that heareth my word, and believeth . . . hath everlasting life and shall not come into condemnation' (John 5:24). His words are 'a lamp unto my feet, and a light unto my path' (Ps. 119:105). They are words of beauty, light, revelation, liberty, joy, forgiveness! Nothing can compare with the transforming words of our Lord Jesus Christ.

The words of Jesus broke the spell of sin and ended an age of darkness. He spoke and demons obeyed his voice. His words still have the power to enthrall us, the power to break the dark night of our sin with the light of his revelation. The words of Jesus bring life!

> There is a Book that through the strife
> Of earth has shown the way of life,
> And marked so plain the open door
> To ways to peace forevermore.
>
> The Book has stood the test of years –
> Has quelled a thousand human fears;
> The Book has given joy for tears,
> God's precious word – the Bible!

This Book, with words of matchless grace,
Unveils to men the Saviour's face;
It tells of Him who bled and died
That our soul-needs may be supplied.

This Book, God's holy word so true,
Has guided men and nations through
The darkest moments ever known.
The way of hope, the Book has shown.

This Book, though threatened ages long,
Still stands in majesty so strong,
Its voice in every clime is heard,
The Book of Books – God's Holy Word!

What wonder there is in the Bible, what power and authority! No other book is like it. In *The Origin of Species* Charles Darwin uses the phrase 'I assume' nearly 3,000 times. In the Bible no such phrase is ever used, but the words 'Thus saith the Lord' is used about 4,000 times! For in Darwin there is no certainty, no assurance; but in the Scriptures we have the certainty of the infallible word of the eternal, infinite God.

So many people have discovered the wonder of Christ's word through the Bible. In the fourth century, St Augustine was a teacher of rhetoric in Milan. He had left home and the influence of his Christian mother, Monica, when still a boy, but he was increasingly dissatisfied with the emptiness of his life and studies. As he sat in his garden one day, deeply depressed in his spirit, he heard a child singing 'Take up and read, take up and read.' At once he went into the house and took up a volume of Paul's Epistles and read the first words that met his eyes: 'Put ye on the Lord Jesus Christ.' At that moment, he said later, 'a light as it were of serenity infused into my heart, all the darkness of doubt vanished away.' Augustine repented, was converted, and became the great teacher of his generation.

Martin Luther, as a young monk in sixteenth century Germany, was depressed by the low moral standards of the Church and the inadequacy of its teachings. In the winter of 1512, as he meditated on Romans 1, he was suddenly gripped by the true meaning of verses 16-17, and realised the liberating truth that God justifies by faith.

John Ruskin, the nineteenth century writer, critic, and an early Utopian socialist, sought constantly for inspiration in the Bible. He wrote, 'It is not only the book of God; it is also the God of books.'

The modern theologian Francis Schaeffer declared, 'He is there and he is not silent.' The God who is there speaks to us; the words of Christ, the living God, carry the divine authority. John Wycliffe said, 'there is only one authority in the Church – that is, Holy Scripture.'

The power and wonder of Christ's words are incomparable. God has 'in these last days spoken unto us by his Son . . . through whom also he created the world. He reflects the glory of God . . . upholding the universe by his word of power' (Heb.1:2-3). Today there are so many wasted and unnecessary words. Politicians, educators, sociologists, philosophers, television commentators, and even many of the clergy, so often talk empty piffle! Recently I had a meal in a restaurant and went off to the washroom to clean up. I was looking for a towel to dry my hands but found one of those hand drying machines instead. I was about to press the button when I noticed a note stuck to the wall above it: 'Please press this button for a recorded message from the Prime Minister' – the point being that what you would get would be nothing but hot air! There is no hot air in the words of Jesus. They are clear and meaningful. They bring light, faith, power, and the answer to our great need in the spiritual darkness of these times.

The fifth century abbot Brendan is said to have been asked by the king, 'What shall I find if I accept your gospel and become Christ's man?' Brendan replied, 'O King, if you become his man you will stumble upon wonder, upon wonder, and every wonder true.' Robert Powell, the actor who played the part of Christ in the film *Jesus of Nazareth* said,

'In portraying Christ I had to confront myself as never before with the question: do I believe? I hadn't been to church since I was a child, and now I had to smother myself in the Bible. I found . . . you can read the words of the Scripture, but when you come to say them aloud it is something different . . . *they are electric!*'

The words of Christ in the Scriptures bring confidence, joy, and power.

The Confidence Of His Words

The Scriptures have the power to bring us confidence. John Wesley gained his confidence as a preacher from the Bible. Though basically a diffident and insecure person, after his conversion he was inspired by the words and example of Christ to join George Whitefield preaching to the crowds in the open in Bristol. He entered the work with some trepidation but found the confidence to proclaim Christ openly, and began his evangelistic journeys that changed the face of the Church in England and brought so many to a personal knowledge of the Lord. Wesley said of the Bible, 'I follow it in all things both great and small.' With the inspiration and confidence that the Scriptures had given him,

Wesley laboured ceaselessly for the Lord, travelling thousands of miles on horseback, preaching thousands of sermons, spending hours in study, reading and writing to God's glory.

Wesley's life is a great example of the dedication and confidence that God's word can inspire. His word brings peace instead of tension, boldness instead of timidity, assurance instead of doubt, forgiveness instead of condemnation.

I have often faced a congregation made up largely of non-Christian people. In the lack of enthusiasm in the singing, in the whole atmosphere, one can feel that these precious people are devoid of any certainty or knowledge of the Lord. Then within an hour everything has changed. The word has come with anointing, Christ's gospel of power has been proclaimed, the crucified and risen Christ has been preached. We know the truth that our great and glorious high priest is interceding for sinners night and day as we see the blind eyes of the congregation opened to the truth of salvation. As the message of Christ and its relevance for their lives reaches them, the whole body of people is transformed. Often whole congregations repent and weep, and sometimes hundreds are born again into Christ in one service. Christ's word brings assurance, confidence, and joy.

'In confidence shall be your strength' (Isa. 30:15). We have boldness, strength and confidence when we know God's commands and follow them. In the old days in Ireland, when only the priest ever read the Scriptures, a priest once caught a peasant reading the Bible. He rebuked him but, with the confidence gained through reading Jesus' words, the peasant said, 'But I have a search warrant to do this.' 'What do you mean?' the priest asked. 'Why, Jesus says "search the Scriptures" and I'm only doing what he tells me!'

The Joy Of His Words

David said: 'I rejoice in your word' (Ps. 119:162). Peter said of Jesus, 'Whom having not seen . . . yet believing, ye rejoice with joy unspeakable' (1 Pet. 1:7-8). When Jesus lived on earth his words brought joy to their hearers: 'The common people heard him gladly' (Mark 12:37). When the disciples had talked to the risen Christ they said, 'Did not our hearts burn within us while he talked with us . . . and opened to us the Scriptures?' (Luke 24:32).

If we take time to read God's word what joys, riches, and satisfaction we will find! It has been said, 'the opposite to joy is not sadness but unbelief.' Belief in Jesus Christ does not bring fleeting happiness; it brings the joy of eternal life. When a people lose touch with God's word they lose peace, satisfaction, and joy.

The Power Of His Words

Recently some 40 famous British personalities, ranging from politicians to royalty to pop stars, were asked to give their favourite Bible passage. It was amazing that the Bible had such an interest for such diverse people, most of whom did not profess to be committed Christians. Here are some of the responses:

Esther Rantzen chose the Book of Esther: the story of a woman who saved a nation.
Jimmy Savile chose Isaiah 9:6-7: the advent of the Prince of Peace.
Margaret Thatcher chose Psalm 46: 'God is our refuge and strength, a very present help in trouble.'
Tony Benn chose Luke 10:22-37: the story of the good Samaritan.

Neil Kinnock chose Ecclesiastes 3:1-12: 'To every thing there is a season.'

Cliff Richard chose Philippians 4:13: 'I can do all things through Christ which strengtheneth me.'

Roger Moore chose 1 Corinthians 13: 'the greatest of these is love.'

Arthur Scargill chose John 2:13-17: Jesus driving the money lenders out of the temple.

George Cole chose Hebrews 13:8: 'Jesus Christ the same yesterday, today, and forever.'

Peter Cushing chose Revelation 21:4: 'And God shall wipe away all tears from their eyes, and there shall be no more death, neither sorrow, nor crying, neither shall there be any more pain: for the former things are passed away.'

It is a proof of the great communicative power of God's word that it can grip the interest of people of such different character and background. What power there is in words for good or evil, for creating or destroying hope! In 1924 Adolf Hitler, a housepainter of obscure Austrian birth, published an autobiographical book *Mein Kampf* (my struggle). It was not taken seriously at the time, but 20 years later millions had died because of the ideas expressed in that book. The power of Hitler's words brought darkness, torment, and suffering to the world. The power of Jesus' words bring light, joy, and peace.

Today multitudes have rejected God's word; it has been banned, ridiculed, or simply ignored. Yet, as H G Wells said, 'The Bible has lost its hold, but nothing has arisen to take its place. This is the gravest aspect of the matter; it was the cement with which our Western communities were built.' Men and women ignored the living Word when he came to earth; today they ignore his written word. You do not have to kill the messenger to silence the truth; it is enough just to be indifferent. Studdert Kennedy illustrated this in one of his poems:

When Jesus came to Birmingham they simply passed him by,
They never hurt a hair of him, they only let him die;
For men had grown more tender, and they would not give him pain,
They only just passed down the street, and left him in the rain.

We neglect God's words to us at our peril, as believers, as individuals, as churches, communities, or nations. The Bible reveals to us God's words, thoughts, and promises, and we cannot know his mind if we do not study his word. Many have sought to destroy the power of the Bible but its words are enshrined in everlasting life and cannot be demolished. It is a resurrection book which rises triumphant from the rubble of modernistic attacks.

To listen to some of the modern theologians and churchmen you would think that God had changed his nature. But God's character is unchanging and unchangeable. His book is unchanged and unchangeable. His power to judge and to save is unchanged and unchangeable. Salvation today is the same as the day that Jesus first preached it. The way to heaven is the same as the day Jesus first preached of it. Hell is the same as the day that Jesus first warned us of it.

Victor Hugo wrote, 'Like the trampling of a mighty army, so is the force of an idea whose time has come.' *God's time has come*. His words are for now, for these trying times. In these dark and difficult days the needs of despairing humankind can be met by the miracle of God's words!

6: *The Miracle of Christ's Conviction*

'Discipleship is a sense of continuous convictions' – Pastor Veyne Austin

I remember being told as a teenager by an old 'ranter' preacher how, when he was a child, he had seen his father negotiating a deal with another businessman at Cardiff Docks. The money involved was £1000 – a huge sum in those days. The money was handed over in cash; there was no receipt, no solicitors, no contract – just a handshake and a promise that the goods would be delivered within two weeks. People used to talk of 'an Englishman's word', in those days. Few are so trustful nowadays but we can still expect God to fulfill his promises. 'God is not a man that he should lie' (Num. 23:19).

God's promises are sure, but they are also sometimes uncomfortable: 'For the word of God is quick and powerful, and sharper than any two-edged sword, piercing even to the dividing asunder of soul and spirit, and of the joints and marrow, and is a discerner of the thoughts and intents of the heart' (Heb. 4:12). It is penetrating, powerful, and often disturbing. The promises of God in his word can hurt. There is something wrong when people sit in church week after week without being cut, convicted, moved by what they hear, and without it changing them.

God's promises reach straight into our souls, and that can be painful. Christ came to awaken and disturb men and women; to shake us from our sins, our self-righteousness, our spiritual lethargy. He disturbed the governments and rulers of his day. He disturbed the priests and pharisees. He disturbed soldiers, lawyers, intellectuals, and multitudes of the common people. Zacchaeus was stirred from his dishonesty into a new life of integrity. The Samaritan woman at the well was pierced by Christ's insight into her impure life and led others to him. His power to convict us of our sins, touch our souls, and change our lives, is the same today.

The Conviction Of The Preachers

Many of the chosen messengers and prophets of God in the Bible were 'put through it' by the Lord. David was convicted from the depth of his soul, crying out, 'Create in me a clean heart, O God, and renew a right spirit within me' (Ps. 51:10). Job heard God speak out of the whirlwind and exclaimed, 'mine eye seeth thee, wherefore I abhor myself, and repent' (Job 42:5-6). Isaiah, under God's conviction, cried, 'I am a man of unclean lips, and I dwell in the midst of a people of unclean lips' (Isa. 6:5). Time after time we read of those who are visited by God falling on their faces, prostrated and humbled by a sense of their own unworthiness.

Preachers today long to see revival but they rely on their own wisdom, personality, and organisation. We may have coachloads of believers going off to rallies and evangelistic meetings, but where are the sinners, the Godless? God is not interested in our organising abilities or our personal charisma. He goes where there is faith. Faith fills our importance with his omnipotence. But there cannot be faith without there first being brokenness. A preacher whose heart has not been broken by God's convicting power will not carry the message of conviction to others.

Tozer said, 'The root of the Church's problem today is compromise.' John F Kennedy was told, as a young politician, 'The way to get along is to go along.' But it is because it has been 'going along' with the world that the Church is now in such great need of restoration. I urge preachers to 'fear no man's censure and crave no man's applause.' Orin Gifford said that when Paul preached it caused either 'riot or a revival.' Revival does not come from a compromised message.

In *A Moveable Feast*, Ernest Hemingway tells how a writer invites his friends to dinner to discuss his latest manuscript. After dinner one after another spoke in glowing praise of the work. The writer listens and announces, 'I shall not send it to the publisher.' His friends are amazed. 'Why? Why not?' they ask. 'If everyone likes it,' the writer says, 'there must be something wrong with it.' *There is something wrong with a message that everyone likes.*

Let us search our hearts. The message cannot be right unless the messenger is right. God has made you; he has loved you from before the world began. If he has called *you* to preach then no one else will do. He is constantly working on our conviction, seeking to draw us, as C S Lewis says, 'farther up and farther in.'

A couple of years ago I was in France, and nothing was going right. I was used to such blessing, such power, such miracles of healing and conversion, but somehow I was failing here. I went into a wood on my own and prayed for hours. God confirmed his calling to me. He gave me peace and assurance but also words of conviction; I wept, repented, and resubmitted myself to his perfect will. That very night the hall was crowded and we began to see miracles again. Hundreds were converted on that tour; a little girl in Nancy who had never walked was running about the packed hall; there were many healing miracles and many convicted. I have never been the same since that touch of the altar of God in a French forest. The preacher must submit to God before the message can be accepted. Let us pray, 'Let me die, Lord, to all self-seeking, self-glorification, self-pity, self-righteousness, self-importance, self-satisfaction.'

The Conviction Of The Message

Christ desires not only to convict the preachers, but the world, through the propagation of his message. There is a great need for an uncompromising emphasis on the fear of God in the message. The gospel message must give people a glimpse of eternity, of heaven and hell. Stephen had such an experience before he died; John had such a revelation. We do not all have supernatural visions, but it is essential that people see the reality of eternity.

The old preachers whom I trained under as a young man were constantly asking the question, 'Where will you spend eternity?' But today, in British churches, the subject of hell is practically taboo. One could visit hundreds of churches on any Sunday without hearing any mention of hell. Yet I regularly speak about hell and I rarely lack a full congregation wherever I preach. Talk of hell does not drive people away; they realise that it is vital and essential doctrine and respond to it.

Our Lord Jesus Christ came to save people from eternal torment; he came 'that whosoever believeth on him should not perish, but have eternal life' (John 3:16). Knowledge of hell was the burning source of Paul's

79

drive to win souls: 'Knowing the terror of the Lord we persuade men' (2 Cor. 5:11). It was behind the intensity of Peter's preaching: '... reserved unto fire against the day of judgment and perdition of ungodly men' (2 Pet. 3:7). It is there in Article 17 of the Church of England: 'God ... hath decreed ... to deliver from curse and damnation those whom he hath chosen in Christ'; it is there in the confessions of faith or articles of faith of all the major Christian denominations. All the great preachers and theologians from Luther to Whitefield to Duncan Campbell have preached of the bottomless pit, the fires of eternity, the furnace of hell.

We must tell people in no uncertain terms that hell is real and it is terrible: a place of anguish, torment, and despair. We must convict people of their sin, and bring them the promise of salvation. We must tell them how Jesus, on the cross, took upon himself our sin, our judgment, our hell; how he paid the price for our sin, went down into the pit for us, and rose again, having ransomed us.

The Conviction Of The People

In Thomas Hardy's short story 'On the Western Circuit', a woman returns from church distressed by a powerful sermon on the evils of drink. Her husband comments, 'It's not much of a sermon if it doesn't hurt'! The conviction of God does hurt. Sometimes there is so much weeping in my services that the seats have to be wiped dry before the next service.

I could tell countless remarkable stories of people convicted by the Holy Spirit. In South Wales some years ago I held a healing crusade where the message of salvation swept the congregation with great power, and many found Jesus. A woman asked to see me after the service. She wept as she confessed to me that she had stolen huge sums of money from the firm she worked for. She was a trusted and respected employee; no one suspected her and there was no way her crime could be discovered. She told me her conscience had never troubled her before, 'until tonight, hearing your message, it all came before me, and I know how wrong I have been.' I had never been faced with such a situation but I knew that the only counsel I could give her was to see her directors and own up. She freely accepted this, courageously facing the possible consequences. She went ahead, and although she had to face a court case, a fine and suspended prison sentence, demotion and lower wages, she now felt that she was at last a free woman.

In New Zealand a well-known television personality came to see me and conviction grew in her as I shared the gospel of our Lord. She was a popular and successful woman but after she had prayed for forgiveness she told me, with tears in her eyes, 'I am going away with more peace than I have ever had before.' At another meeting a woman was so angered by the message that she stormed out and drove the 20 miles to her home. She went to bed, but was so disturbed that she could not sleep. In the middle of the night she drove back to see the pastor and his wife, and before the day dawned she had knelt, weeping, to give her life to God.

People have described God's work of conviction in different ways. Paul Yonggi Cho calls it 'the unrelenting pressure of God', whereas Kathryn Kuhlman speaks of God as 'a gentleman', gently but persistently reminding us where our needs can be met. David Pawson referred to God's convicting work as 'the daddy longlegs of the Church', moving around quietly and subtly.

However God brings about conviction, whether in dramatic conversion or subtle pressure, he always calls for a response from us. Fred Lemon was a convicted criminal in prison when he had a vision of Jesus, resulting in a miraculous conversion, and a great witness for Christ. Saul responded to his experience on the Damascus road and his life was changed. The Philippian jailor responded to the earthquake in the prison (Acts 16) by crying, 'What must I do to be saved?', the same question that the people asked when Peter preached. I remember when I was preaching once, the convicting power of the Holy spirit had swept over the meeting, and a man in the congregation stood up and shouted, 'What must I do to get it then?'

Not all conversions are dramatic. Sometimes it is a slow, quiet, progressive experience. C S Lewis took years to become a Christian. He fought against belief until, one day, on the top of a bus in Oxford he realised that he was holding back and 'gave in and admitted that God was God'. It took another year of God's 'celestial interference' before he surrendered completely and acknowledged Jesus as Lord. The Russian writer Alexander Solzhenitsyn, in a Stalinist forced labour camp, read the rough handwritten Scriptures that circulated secretly in the camp and, after much thought, gradually surrendered to Christ. Malcolm Muggeridge felt a growing dislike of the destructiveness of modern society, and after years of thought and discussion, and finally a visit to Mother Teresa, he eventually grasped hold of what he called 'the real Jesus'.

Many people have told me that, after being in a meeting where the power of God was manifest, they went home and found themselves somehow different. Without their being consciously 'converted', God's presence remained with them, and they found they could not smoke, go to the pub, swear. The work of conviction had taken hold of them and would not let them go. God calls us through Christ in a stunning and powerful way: 'Cast away from you all your transgressions . . . and make you a new heart and a new spirit, for why will ye die. . .?' (Ezek. 18:31).

The Conviction Of The Heart

What are the elements of true conviction? Jesus said that when the Holy spirit came, 'he will convince the world of sin and of righteousness and of judgment' (John 16:8-9 RSV). We have to know what is wrong with us before we can put it right.

I am driving with my wife when she says, 'you should have taken that turning on the right that we just passed.' 'No,' I say confidently, 'I know this road – we don't turn off for another mile yet.' My wife tries to insist but I am adamant, certain that I am right and she is wrong. I keep driving but gradually realise that the road looks unfamiliar, the turn off is a long time coming. My wife is silent but the conviction grows that she was right and I was wrong. Finally, ten miles along the wrong road I swallow my pride and turn back. At last we see the turning my wife had indicated. There it is, properly signposted, but I can not accept that it is the right way until I have accepted that I have been going the wrong way.

We can always depend on God to direct us in life and show us when we are on the wrong road. Just as a doctor can show us on an X-ray what is wrong with our body and what might need removing, God will point out what is wrong or unhealthy in our lives and needs changing. God convicts our hearts by warning, speaking, enlightening us.

Conviction can have no long-term effect on a person's life unless it is followed by repentance. The Scripture demands it, justice requires it, Christ preached it, God expects it. Repentance is not just sorrow for our sins; it involves an about turn, a decision to abandon our past and dedicate ourselves to a new future. Repentance is costly.

Savonarola, the great fifteenth century Italian religious reformer, shook Florence by his powerful and uncompromising preaching of the gospel. When the great but oppressive ruler Lorenzo de Medici lay dying, convicted of his sin, he called for Savonarola to hear his confession. The preacher came, and offered Lorenzo absolution on three conditions. 'First, you must repent.' Lorenzo accepted this. 'Second, you must give up your ill-gotten wealth.' With some hesitation, Lorenzo reluctantly agreed. 'Third, you must restore the liberties of Florence.' Lorenzo would not accept this and Savonarola left him, soon to die unabsolved. True repentance demands reparation for sin.

Repentance requires humility, but it also requires courage. It can be a heroic resolve, an act that breaks the chains of captive and oppressed souls. God comes with clear guidance showing us what is wrong and how to repent. 'The goodness of God leadeth thee to repentance' (Rom. 2:4).

God guides us from conviction to repentance to a true change of heart and life. Changed lives are the fruits of conviction. Paul says that God has 'saved us by the washing of regeneration, and renewing of the Holy Ghost' (Titus 3:5). Regeneration means new birth, the changing and renovation of the soul by the Spirit and grace of God.

The prodigal son was convicted of his wickedness when he was feeding the swine – he realised he was in the wrong place. Then he repented, he 'came to himself' and was sorry for his sin. Lastly he brought about a changed life by returning to his father, confessing, and accepting forgiveness.

The miracle of conviction is God's power and ability to show us what we are, where we are, where we need to go. It is a miracle for a sinner to be brought into harmony with the living God. The Christian life starts with conviction and continues with convictions as God guides us through the path of discipleship.

7: The Miracle of Christ's Cross

It is the divine humility . . .

C S Lewis

The nineteenth century Christian philanthropist Quintin Hogg, who founded the first polytechnic in London in the 1860s, to provide education for poor boys, was asked what it cost to build the institute. He replied, 'Only one man's lifeblood.' There was one who literally gave his lifeblood for the perfect and eternal salvation of the human race.

A few years ago an airlane crew were crossing the Atlantic when their aircraft developed serious engine trouble. They could not reach land and were losing height when, in the sky ahead, they saw a burning cross. It went before them for several miles; the plane began to steady and the pilot gained control. The cross went before them until they landed safely and then vanished. The pilot later told reporters, 'I can never be the same again. Every time I see a cross I shall remember that I was saved by a cross.'

We are saved by a cross. That is the central theme of the Christian faith. With that message the early believers turned the world upside down, and it was the essence of Paul's teaching: 'The preaching of the cross is . . . the power of God' (1 Cor. 1:18); 'I determined not to know anything among you, save Jesus Christ, and him crucified' (1 Cor. 2:2).

In the church of St Maria degli Angioli in Lugano, the wonderful frescoes of Bernardino Luini can be seen. The whole ceiling is covered with the representation of the Passion and right in the middle is the cross, with Christ seeming to bear down upon the world, lifted high. One's overwhelming impression is that he is the pre-eminence – the central challenge – and one remembers, 'I, if I be lifted up from the earth, will draw all men unto me' (John 12:32).

There is power enough in the blood shed on the cross to cleanse the whole world of sin. The glorious work of Calvary is amazing in its effect on men and women. Noel Proctor, the prison chaplain who has seen so many miracles of Christ's redeeming power among hardened criminals in Strangeways Prison, told the story of one particularly hard and vicious man. He had been involved with the occult and was aggressive towards Noel, but one day he wandered into the prison chapel and saw the cross illuminated in the stained glass window. He fell on his face beneath it weeping. The very sight of the cross had broken one of the hardest of men. 'Christ died for the ungodly' (Rom. 5:6); 'Who is he that condemneth? It is Christ that died' (Rom. 8:34).

Calvary was the greatest sermon Jesus ever preached. Thank God for Golgotha; thank God for his suffering and death; thank God that he went down into hell and defeated principalities and powers; thank God that he rose again and we are saved because of his blood shed for us. 'Neither by the blood of goats and calves, but by his own blood, he . . . obtained redemption for us' (Heb. 9:12). There is only one sacrifice: the atonement procured on the cross, which alone can save, heal, empower, cleanse, and uplift our broken lives. So many have witnessed this truth: Isabel Chapman saw it in amazing miracles among the headhunting tribes of the Philippines; David Wilkerson saw it on the streets of New York and Chicago as hardened young criminals were won; Jackie Pullinger is seeing it as hundreds of drug addicts and pushers are transformed by the blood of Jesus.

I have witnessed it as I have seen thousands caught up in the healing revolution; as I have lifted up the cross and seen healing for their wounds and diseases. As I have uplifted the cross the broken-hearted have been restored and lives marred by sin remade. As I have uplifted the cross the blind have seen, the deaf heard, the paralysed have run, and cancers have withered. As I have uplifted the cross a multitude have found peace of heart and mind.

From the cross Jesus joined hands with every repentant sinner, as the Passover lamb was slain, to rise on the third day as our Redeemer and Lord. The atonement is the perfect plan whereby a sinner may be reconciled to God. Yet this truth arouses great hostility. Billy Sunday used to say, 'More battles have been fought over the cross than any other Christian issue . . .' George Bernard Shaw said once, 'I hate this blood sacrifice for man's sin – it is diabolical.' Other religions seek to undermine the significance of the crucifixion. The Koran says, 'We believe in Allah and that which has been revealed to us and that which was revealed to Abraham, and Ishmael and Isaac and Jacob and the tribes, and that which was given to Moses and Jesus, and that which was given to the prophets from their Lord, we do not make any distinction between any of them' (2:136). They make no distinction between the spotless Son of God, our saviour, and mere men – good and holy men perhaps, but still sinful mortal men.

In the United Nations building in New York a small

room was put aside for prayer. Some Christian employees wanted to put a cross on the wall, but their request was rejected as it was thought it might give offence to other religions. The cross gives offence to many; it is 'a stumbling block' as Paul said. The old hymn says:

> What can wash away my sin
> Nothing but the blood of Jesus

The Jesus I hold up in my crusades is the crucified bleeding Jesus, God's ultimatum to sin, for 'without shedding of blood is no remission' (Heb. 9:23). But the crucified Jesus is despised and rejected. The cross was the symbol of shame to the people of Christ's day, and to many still it seems so unlovely, so forlorn and futile, that they cannot accept it as central to God's plan. The Welsh preacher Eric Dando once said, 'It was the most unusual place that you could have expected God to meet the need of a dying, thirsty humanity.'

God could have used any way of redeeming us, but he chose the cross. The Second World War poet, Alun Lewis, wrote, 'By what mysterious alchemy could God so fashion materials as this, to make them the pivot of his plans?' But the rough wood of the cross, the piercing nails, were the emblems of Christ's greatness, his humility, obedience and love, materials transformed by the Father into glorious victory.

The cross is the foundation stone of Christianity. When some Christian missionaries visited Mahatma Gandhi he asked them, before they left, to sing him one of their songs. 'Which one?' they asked, and Gandhi replied, 'Sing the one which best expresses what you believe.' They sang:

When I survey the wondrous cross
On which the prince of glory died,
My richest gain I count but loss,
And pour contempt on all my pride.

When we gaze at Calvary we see the very summit of
Christ's greatness, the very purpose of his life, his glory,
his magnificence, the proof of his love for us. John said,
Jesus Christ . . . loved us and washed us from our sins
in his own blood' (Rev. 1:5). His love shone forth to the
whole world. A little boy who had come as an orphan
to a Spurgeon's Children's Home was asked by the
housemother if he liked the chapel there. 'Yes, I do,' the
child replied, 'I like that big kiss on the wall.' The cross
is the symbol of God's love to a loveless world.

In Tibet the shepherds build small stone enclosures
and each night place one small lamb inside. If a wolf
comes at night it smells the lamb and, instead of
attacking the main flock, squeezes into the enclosure to
kill and eat it. But the wolf is trapped, it cannot get out,
and in the morning it is killed by the shepherds. One
lamb is sacrificed to save the other sheep. Jesus, the
lamb of God, died to save his sheep. ' We have redemption through his blood.'

If it were not for Calvary Satan would have had the
victory. But Jesus gave himself as a ransom for many.
For you and me he endured the shame, the suffering,
the agony of the cross, and for that reason he is worthy
to bruise Satan's head. Satan was defeated at the cross;
he cannot touch the believing soul who is protected by
the blood of Calvary. The cross gives the Christian
power to defeat the evil one: 'Greater is he that is in you
than he that is in the world' (1 John 4:4).

When Jesus cried, 'It is finished' he completed his
work forever. David Watson said, 'It was the greatest

word ever uttered.' Christ's work was completed, consummated, fulfilled; it need never be repeated or added to. That one transaction was enough once and forever to put an end to suffering, sin, and death, and to deal the death blow to Satan, the accuser and enemy of our souls. The Greek word used in the Scripture, *tetelestai*, means 'accomplished'. If you go to Greece for a holiday you may find that when you pay your hotel bill it is stamped with a word which has just the same root: it's implication is that the transaction is completed, there is nothing more to pay!

'He hath made him to be sin for us, who knew no sin' (2 Cor. 5:21). For it was your sin and mine that put Christ on the cross. You and I gave him a crown of thorns, but he gives us a crown of righteousness. You and I gave him a cross to carry, but he gives us a yoke which is easy. You and I put nails in his hands, but he delivers us safely into the Father's hands. You and I gave him a mocking title, but he gives us a new name written down in glory. You and I stripped him of his clothes, but he gives us the garments of salvation. You and I gave him vinegar to drink, but he gives us the living water. Your sinfulness and mine put him on the tree, but his sinlessness puts us into a place of grace.

Because of Christ's sacrifice for us we can come to him lost and be found, come to him sick and be healed, come to him a sinner and be made a saint! I have seen so many sick and sinful people radiantly transformed at the foot of the cross. I knew a man who was known in his town as 'the wild man'. He was violent, a drunkard and wife-beater, a regular occupant of the police cells. That man heard the gospel message of Christ's redeeming blood and by God's grace his life was changed.

Today he is an evangelist, known in his town as 'the wonder man'.

The death of Christ was vital for the whole human race, the most significant event of human history. If you read biographies of great men and women you will find only a tiny proportion of the book dealing with the person's death. Yet in the Gospels the death of Christ is considered the most important aspect of his life. In the Gospels of Matthew and Mark one third of the books are about Jesus' death, in Luke one quarter, and in John almost half. Jesus came to earth with the purpose of dying, to save his people from their sins. On the hill of Calvary he suffered torture for us. Battered, bruised, bleeding, broken, he gave up his lifeblood for the very people who had hated and persecuted him and prayed, 'Father, forgive them, for they know not what they do.' He secured our eternal salvation, undeserving, rebellious, indifferent as we are. The righteous died for the unrighteous, the just for the unjust, the sinless for the sinful.

Jesus died on the cross for each one of us, regardless of our status. Bishop Stephen Bayne wrote:

I remember one Sunday morning when my eyes turned to the long row of people kneeling at the communion rail. For some reason I began looking at the soles of their shoes. And it was an extraordinarily moving sight to me, even then. These people, so many of whom I knew as giants, and people of importance in the congregation, were amazingly and secretly different when you saw the soles of their shoes. And there was a sort of anonymity about it, with the moving reflection of new shoes revealed next to old shoes. There were holes in some shoes . . . some were large, some small, some stylishly narrow, some broad and heavy.

The significance of this experience was that the ground of the cross is level ground. All must kneel before the crucified Christ. At the foot of the cross there is equality.

There are no pretensions at the foot of the cross. In the words of the old song we must come:

> Just as I am – without one plea
> But that thy blood was shed for me

There is a story of a famous artist who met an old, ragged, filthy tramp, and asked him if he would model for him. He gave him the address of his studio and promised him a good fee. The next day the tramp turned up, but he had cleaned himself up, washed and shaved, and put on some decent clothes. The artist said, 'No, that won't do. I wanted you just as you were.' We cannot put on a veneer of cleanness, display our religion and righteousness, and try to prove our worthiness. We must come to the cross just as we are, sinful and unworthy as we are. The cross is sufficient to meet us.

In the Rocky Mountains there is a place called the Great Divide. Waters flow down the steep, rocky cliffsides into a deep ravine. Soon the fast flowing stream becomes divided; the waters on one side flow across the country, eventually to empty into the warm waters of the Pacific, while the waters of the other side flow in the opposite direction towards the Atlantic. The cross of Christ is the great divide. We can accept it or reject it. We are either for it or against it, gathered to him or scattered abroad, sheep or goats. We have a choice.

If we accept Christ's redemption, accept life instead of death, then we share in the glory that he won with his blood. Today we wait in the wings, but one day we shall take our place with our glorious Redeemer, in the full spotlight of his glory. *That is the miracle of his cross!*

8: The Miracle of Christ's Resurrection

Alive! Forever more He lives!
Enthroned on high;
Conqueror of death's domain,
With heavenly light and hope
He fills the hearts of men.

A E Fletcher

The philosopher Professor C E M Joad was a regular panel member of the popular BBC Radio programme *The Brains Trust*, on which the panel discussed topics and questions suggested by listeners. They were once asked: if you could ask one question of any person living or dead, what would the question be and of whom would you ask it? Joad, at that time an agnostic, unhesitatingly replied, 'I would ask Jesus Christ if he actually rose from the dead, because the truth of this matter is of paramount importance.' This was a perceptive answer because the Resurrection of Jesus is the bed-rock on which the edifice of Christianity rests. As Paul observed, 'If Christ be not raised your faith is in vain, ye are yet in your sins' (1 Cor. 15:17), but he continues (v.20) triumphantly, 'But now is Christ risen.' Happily, Professor Joad came to accept that statement; after writing his last book *Return to the Faith* he died a Christian.

Many people know that the facts and details of the Resurrection are to be found in the Gospels, but do not realise that further evidence is provided in the Book of Acts. This book was written by Luke as a sequel to his Gospel, and he begins by referring to the earlier work as dealing with, 'all that Jesus *began* both to do and teach, until the day in which he was taken up.' Luke's Gospel ends with the risen Christ ascending into heaven, and Acts begins at this point. The risen Jesus, who had shown himself alive to his apostles, would now show himself alive from his throne in heaven.

This difference between the Christ of the Gospels and the Christ of Acts has great significance for us. A minister once announced that his sermon would be about the 29th chapter of Acts. His congregation looked for the place in their Bibles but of course found that there are only 28 chapters in the book. Smiling at their confusion, the minister told them that *they* were the 29th chapter. The Book of Acts is still being written. The Gospels record the coming of the Saviour and the triumphant conclusion of his redeeming work: 'It is finished,' as Jesus cried from the cross. The Gospels all end with the word *Amen*, but the Book of Acts does not.

C S Lewis said of the resurrected Christ, 'He has met, fought, and beaten the King of death; everything is different because he has done so, this is the beginning of a new creation.' The Acts record the ongoing manifestation of the risen Christ in his Church, and the proofs found in the book will be those seen in the Church today. If we can recognise those same proofs in our midst we are enabled to 'give a reason of the hope that is in us' (1 Pet. 3:15).

The Risen Lord Answers Prayer

The first act of the apostles was to fill the vacancy left by the defection and death of Judas. They cast lots after praying, 'Thou, Lord, which knowest the hearts of all men, show whether of these two thou hast chosen' (Acts 1:24). It was as though they felt that Jesus was present as truly as he was when he called them to follow him beside the sea of Galilee.

Many prayers are recorded in the Book of Acts for all kinds of needs – healing, raising the dead, the infilling of the Holy Spirit, deliverance from prison – and many remarkable answers to prayer were received. It is futile to talk to a corpse, so if talking to Jesus receives a response he cannot be dead. Answer to prayer is evidence of his Resurrection.

The Risen Lord Sent His Holy Spirit

The second chapter of Acts records how, at Pentecost, the Holy Spirit came as a rushing mighty wind and appearedd to them as 'cloven tongues like as of fire.' This coming of the Holy Spirit was promised by Jesus before his death (John 14:16-17,26; 15:26; 16:7). On the evening of his Resurrection day, he appeared to the disciples and breathed on them, saying, 'Receive ye the Holy Ghost' (John 20:22), demonstrating that he was the source of the Spirit. And before his ascension he promised the disciples that they should 'wait for the promise of the Father' and they would 'receive power after that the Holy Ghost is come upon you' (Acts 1:4,8). Now he had ascended he kept his promise and Pentecost was the result. People going on holiday often promise friends that they will send them a postcard; the card is proof that they arrived, that they are really there at the resort.

So the Pentecostal experience reminds us that Jesus has 'arrived', he is on his throne. As Peter preached in his Pentecost sermon, 'Jesus . . . being by the right hand of God exalted, and having received of the Father the promise of the Holy Ghost, he hath shed forth this, which ye now see and hear' (Acts 2:32-33). This experience of baptism in the Spirit was accompanied by speaking in tongues, at Pentecost (Acts 2:6), with Cornelius and his household (10:46), at Ephesus (19:6). Every time we speak in tongues, or see any manifestation of the Spirit's outpouring, we have further proof of Christ's Resurrection.

The Risen Lord Changes Lives

The Book of Acts records many incidents of individuals, families, and communities whose lives are changed by their turning to Christ. Saul, the persecuter of the Church, is dramatically arrested by the risen Christ on the Damascus road. The eunuch returning to Ethiopia encounters the evangelist Philip and becomes a Christian. Cornelius, a Roman centurion, and all his household turn to Christ. Lydia, a successful businesswoman, becomes Europe's first convert. The small group of believers at the beginning of the book is now numbered in thousands as the gospel net is spread wider and wider. Jesus said, 'I will build my Church' (Matt. 16:18). That is what he was doing at the time of Acts and that is what he is still doing. When sinners turn to Christ in repentance and are born again it is further proof that he is risen.

Conversion and resurrection are closely related. The gospel message is one of rebirth from the spiritual grave to which our sin and guilt have brought us. Christians are 'those who are alive from the dead' (Rom. 6:13), restored to new life in fellowship with God. We are quickened from death, raised to life, exalted to heaven. This is a miracle – as supernatural an event as the resurrection of the body. Graham Kendrick's song says:

> Now the fear of death is broken,
> Love has won the crown,
> Prisoners of the darkness listen,
> Walls are tumbling down

New birth in Christ frees us from the bondage of sin and opens up possibilities that were formally impossible. The Resurrection calls us into an experience with the living God that enables us to leave the lowlands of selfishness, greed, injustice, and misery, and rise into the uplands of faith, love, reverence, and praise. Confidence in the resurrected Lord, death's conqueror, brings freedom from all fear.

When General Allenby's forces captured Jerusalem in the First World War, the defeated Turks hastened to the famous tomb of Jesus and, as a dispatch recorded, 'robbed it of its treasures'. But Allenby commented, 'It's not true. It was robbed of its treasure 2,000 years ago when Jesus rose again, conquered death, and walked out of it forever! Hallelujah!' Our greatest treasure is the sure knowledge that Jesus 'was raised again for our justification' (Rom. 4:25).

The Risen Lord Brings Healing

The Christ who, while on earth, healed in so many different ways, now heals through his disciples. We see this first in Acts when Peter commands healing for the crippled man who begged outside the temple gate. There was more than just healing involved in this incident. A man 'lame from his mother's womb' immediately walked, danced, and leaped without having first to learn the techniques. Dorcas was dead but Peter's prayer restored her to life. Another such miracle was the raising of Eutychus (Acts 20:7-12), the young man who fell asleep during a very long sermon of Paul's. He 'dropped off' literally, falling down from his third-storey window seat and fatally injuring himself, but Paul restored him. The people of Lystra witnessed a miracle of healing (Acts 14) and, in their ignorance, thought that Paul and Barnabus were the gods Mercury and Jupiter. The apostles were horrified and were quick to assure the people that they were ordinary people like themselves, and indeed, in all these healings the apostles were only the channels. It was the risen Christ who performed the miracles. And it is the same today with those followers of Jesus who act as channels of his healing power.

I recently held a mission in a small West Country town and we were blessed with wonderful miracles. Perhaps the one that had the most impact on the town was the healing of a man who had Parkinson's disease. He had come to the meeting on two sticks but he left it running. The meeting was just before Easter and he said that he would always link his new life with the new life of the first Easter Day. Not long after, he met an old friend in the town, the local undertaker, who immediately noticed the change in him and said, 'I thought you were soon going to be one of my customers but I see you have had a resurrection!'

When we pray to Jesus and people are healed, it is yet another proof of his Resurrection. We need to remind people today that the Scripture is still true: 'He who raised Christ Jesus from the dead will give life to your mortal bodies also' (Rom. 8:11 RSV). Let us tell this dark, defeated generation, torn by so much fear, stress, and conflict, that *Jesus Christ rose from the dead to heal us*, and that we can know his dynamic power in the divine healing of afflicted bodies and minds.

The Risen Lord Changes Society

We see the reforming power of the risen Lord from the time of Acts and throughout history. Barriers between Jew and Gentile are broken down when Peter is directed to take the Good News to the Roman centurion Cornelius. We see how the Lord influences civilisation in Paul's being directed, by divine intervention, to Macedonia. As a result it is now Europe, rather than Asia Minor, that has a Christian culture and heritage.

The risen Christ exerts the same influence on society today. We see the proof of his power in so many ways. The Christ who attacked bigotry and injustice has worked to change society through such Christian reformers as William Wilberforce, Elizabeth Fry, and Lord Shaftesbury. Christian missionaries have brought peace and stability to many lands. The medical and educational services owe their origins to the Church. Christ's impact on the moral, physical, and mental wellbeing of the human race is proof of his Resurrection.

We see the power of the risen Lord in the events of history. We see the enemies of the Lord defeated many times in the Book of Acts: Herod dies before he can fulfil his plans to kill Peter; the apostles are arrested and imprisoned on several occasions, but this is used as an opportunity to defeat the authorities and provide opportunities for the gospel to be preached. And we see Christ's enemies defeated in many of the events of more recent history: from the conquering of empty religion and superstition by the Reformation to the defeat of Nazism and the formation of the State of Israel.

When Christ's enemies persecuted the Church at Jerusalem they in fact encouraged the spread of Christianity as the disciples scattered far and wide, spreading the gospel. And we still see enemies of the Church 'hoist with their own petard'. Even before it became a Communist country, China was a country where missionary work was extremely difficult. Christian missionaries were hindered by the lack of proper roads, the number of different dialects spoken, and the tradition whereby people's families were always consulted before any decision was taken, which meant that potential converts were often discouraged. When the Communists took over they expelled the missionaries and set about reforming the country. They eventually brought about the general education of the people in a single dialect, the practice of individual decision making, and the building of efficient roads and railways. Now that the situation has eased somewhat and China is becoming open to missionaries again, they find that their previous problems have been resolved. Just as God used the Egyptians to educate Moses for their own destruction, he has used Communists to advance his cause in China.

The recent nuclear accident at Chernobyl in the Soviet Union appears to many to have the mark of the risen Christ upon it. This appalling disaster is expected to bring about a total of almost 50,000 deaths, and of course food and water supplies over a vast area have been poisoned. The word *chernobyl* means 'wormwood' and the site of the nuclear power station was named because this plant is grown in the area. Revelation 8:10-11 reads:

There fell a great star from heaven, burning as it were a lamp, and it fell upon the third part of the rivers, and upon the fountain of waters, and the name of the star is called Wormwood, and the third part of the waters became wormwood, and many men died of the waters because they were made bitter.

The connection between this prophecy and the Chernobyl disaster has not been lost on Soviet citizens and many have turned to the Bible. In an officially atheist state, events have compelled people to consider God's word, and no one can begin to calculate how that might effect the Soviet Union.

The Risen Lord Gives Us Hope Of Heaven

Death is our enemy, but Jesus has robbed the grave of its victory. Among the many moving stories that emerged from the Nuremberg war trials in 1946 was one of a pregnant young Jewish woman who was being hunted by the Gestapo. She fled into a graveyard and, seeing a freshly-dug empty grave, slipped down into it. She eluded the Nazi soldiers but was then unable to climb out of the grave. She settled there for the night but her labour began and during the night she gave birth, delivering her son herself. The gravedigger, a Jew who had managed to conceal his race from the Nazis, found them in the morning and exclaimed, 'It must be the Messiah! Only the Messiah could come out of a tomb.' Jesus is the Messiah who came out of the tomb to change death to victory!

Jesus told his disciples:

Let not your heart be troubled ... In my Father's house are many mansions ... I go to prepare a place for you. And if I go to prepare a place for you, I will come again and receive you unto myself; that where

I am, there you may be also . . . because I live ye shall live also (John 14:1-3,19).

As Paul says, 'We know that if our earthly house of this tabernacle were dissolved, we have a building of God, a house not made with hands, eternal in the heavens' (2 Cor. 5:1). Stephen, dying at the hands of his enemies, had a glimpse of the resurrected Lord triumphant over death. He looked up and 'saw Jesus standing at the right hand of God' (Acts 7:55). Jesus has killed death and given us, as our goal, not the grave but the glory. He 'shall change our vile body, that it may be fashioned like unto his glorious body' (Phil. 4:21). I often tell my wife that I shall be handsome one day!

Jesus' Resurrection frees us forever from the fear of death. As Charles Wesley wrote:

> Vain the stone, the watch, the seal;
> Christ hath burst the gates of hell:
> Death in vain forbids his rise;
> Christ hath opened paradise.
>
> Lives again our glorious King!
> Where, O death, is now thy sting?
> Once he died our souls to save:
> Where thy victory, O grave?

The Resurrection is, as Abraham Lincoln once said, 'the best proven fact in history'. From the time of the early Church, throughout history, and today, we see constant evidence of the risen Lord: in answered prayer, in healing, in the baptism of the Holy Spirit, in changes in the lives of individuals and societies. Above all, the Resurrection gives us hope. Bramwell Booth said that the name of the risen Jesus was 'a name to live by and a name to die by'. Trust in the Resurrection and live for Christ risen. And in the drifting winds of uncertainty, the storms of darkness, and the fogs of doubt that assail us, we can be sure that the risen Lord will be at our side, and be there to welcome us when we reach eternity. Then we shall see him face to face, believe, and live forever through the miracle of the Resurrection.

9: *The Miracle of Christ's Second Coming*

'It is later than you think' – Ronald Reagen

The Duke of Edinburgh said recently that he had nightmares when he thought of the world's future. This is indeed a dark and despairing world and to many it seems that darker days are coming, and that the course of this world has not long to run. In *The Tempest* Shakespeare writes of a disappearing world:

> The cloud-capped towers, the gorgeous palaces,
> The solemn temples, the great globe itself.
> Yea, all which it inherit, shall dissolve
> And, like this insubstantial pageant faded,
> Leave not a rack behind . . .

The Bible too speaks of the earth 'dissolving' (2 Pet. 3:10-11), and the prophecies of Revelation seem to be more relevant than ever before.

We Know That A Judgment Is Coming

We cannot know exactly when it will be, but we can be sure that this world will end one day and that a great judgment will follow: 'He hath appointed a day, in the which he shall judge the world' (Acts 17:31).

105

Recently a national newspaper asked some well-known personalities if they thought that there would be a judgment day. The stage star Jessie Matthews said, 'I think man will pay for his wrongdoing in the end.' The racing driver Graham Hill said, 'I believe the fate of the world is in our hands; we will make our own judgment, our own hell and heaven on earth.' Other answers ranged from, 'God will be merciful to us all in the end' to 'I've never given it a thought'! No doubt every person one asked would give a different answer. But the Bible makes it clear that judgment will come: 'It is appointed unto men once to die, but after this the judgment' (Heb. 9:27).

The Bible actually speaks of five different judgments: the judgment of nations in the valley of Jehoshaphat (Joel 3:12-14); the judgment of angels (Jude v.6); the judgment of Jerusalem, or of the chosen race of Jews (Ezek. 14:21-23); the 'judgment seat of Christ' (Rom. 14:10; 2 Cor. 5:10); the great judgment of all before the 'great white throne' (Rev. 20:11-15). We do not know if these judgments mentioned are all one or are distinct. Certainly we know that God has given his Son 'authority to execute judgment' (John 5:27); Jesus said, 'For judgment am I come into the world' (John 9:39).

Paul asks, 'Thinkest thou . . . that thou shall escape the judgment of God?' (Rom. 2:3). Many have hoped to do so, like Adolf Eichmann, one of the most wicked perpetrators of the Holocaust, who was eventually tried for his war crimes in Israel in 1961. He was found guilty and sentenced to death. Before his execution he requested that when he was dead his body should be burned and the ashes scattered into the Mediterranean Sea. When asked his reason he replied, 'so that I might escape the judgment of God.' How foolish! Revelation

20:13 says, 'and the sea gave up the dead which were in it.'

A young Christian was talking to a businessman, and trying to persuade him to come to church and hear the gospel. The man said that he could not go to church on a Sunday: 'I spend the day settling my accounts.' The Christian replied, 'And so shall God settle accounts with you on the day of judgment.' That day is surely coming, and Jesus has said, 'Whosoever shall deny me before men, him will I also deny before my Father which is in heaven' (Matt. 10:33).

People think that they can get away with their sins, that they aren't so bad really. 'There are plenty worse than me,' they tell me, 'You ought to see some of the people in my office, my factory . . . lots of people sin all the time and nothing happens to them, they get away with it . . .' No one gets away with it! When you push your trolley round the supermarket you pick up a tin here, a packet there, some cheese from this shelf, some meat from that, and finally head towards the door. But before you get out you are stopped by the checkout – the accounting place. You cannot leave until you have paid for all you have collected in your trolley. The wise Preacher said: 'Walk in the ways of thine heart, and in the sight of thine eyes, but know thou that for all these things God will bring thee into judgment' (Eccles. 11:9).

The Darkness Of The World

There is no doubt that we are living in dark days. We see the galloping horsemen of the Apocalypse: the white horse of deception, the red horse of war, the black horse of famine and want, the pale horse of death. In an age of wealth and materialism we see hunger and misery. Nations are torn by war and, despite the new Soviet image of *glasnost* and overtures of friendship, the Soviet bloc are still piling up their armaments and the threat of nuclear war still looms.

In the affluent West we live in an age of uncertainty and of greed. We live in an age where people are hungering, not after righteousness, but after sin. This lax, licentious age, where money is god and drunkenness and divorce tear families apart, is deceiving millions. They are being prepared for the coming of the antichrist. People think they are seeking security but they are lured by the impermanent, the unstable, and unreliable. The claims of Christ are met by scoffing and hostility, by indifference, or by sophisticated and arrogant rejection.

When I walk in the Wiltshire countryside I often see signs saying 'Trespassers will be prosecuted'. Many have trespassed from God's way, disregarding his commandments, breaking his code of morality, holiness, and righteousness. Many too have trespassed onto forbidden territory that belongs to God. We see people ruined by devious cults, burdened and crushed by false doctrines. The legions of hell are great!

The Coldness Of The Church

'Judgment must begin at the house of God' (1 Pet. 4:17). Jeremiah cried, 'the turtle and the crane and the swallow observe the time of their coming, but my people know not the judgment of the Lord' (Jer. 8:7). Many Christians have become sedated by the world and its addictions, by television and video, pleasure-seeking, money and material things. In spite of world-wide evangelism only a few are entering in at the narrow gate. *The Church is asleep and does not hear the enemy at the gate!*

We see around us the break-up of family life, the lusting for new partners and financial gain, and Christians are not immune to the lure of worldliness. We see sorrow and despair walking our streets but the Church is lukewarm and uncaring. In Britain in particular the Church is asleep. While churches and ministers throughout the world respond with enthusiasm to our offer of an evangelistic team with a proved and reputable record of evangelism and church-building, in Britain the general response is one of apathy and indifference. In spite of so-called 'renewal' the fiery evangelism of the past, dedicated to the winning of the lost, is hardly to be found in our churches.

Our days are numbered. God is calling the bride but many are contaminated and tainted by the darkness of the world. The Church needs to see true repentance and restoration, true lamentation as we shake off the entanglements of worldliness and prepare to meet the King. If we are committed to him he will cover us and shield us when the great day of judgment comes. Let us not be ashamed before our Lord when we face eternity.

We have a message to take from the throne, a warning to the nation, but those who should take it to them are all too often mesmerised by the comfortable prophets of our time. Winston Churchill said many years ago, 'the tide of immorality that has swept the land is due to the fact that no longer is hell and judgment preached from the pulpits of the churches.' J B Phillips, the theologian and Bible translator, said, 'There is too much . . . sentimental Christianity, too much of God's love and not enough of his judgment.' I am glad that I have been able to share the message of the second coming of Christ, and his judgment, with so many people in my lifetime. I make it a vital point of every crusade to preach this subject and remind people of the day that is to come. Many who entered a service hard and unrepentant have wept before the Lord as this glorious truth is revealed, they have found the living God and are now ready for that day.

Let it not be said of us, 'My people have changed their glory for that which doth not profit' (Jer. 2:11). Let us live as servants in the household of faith, living holy, consecrated lives and trusting in God. Let us carry the gospel to every city, every town, every village and hamlet. Each morning when I wake I praise God for a new day and say, 'God is delaying the judgment, that we may bring more people to repentance, deliver them from their fears, and prepare them for his coming.'

The Hope Of The True Church

The angels told the disciples, 'This same Jesus, which is taken up from you into heaven, shall so come in like manner as ye have seen him go into heaven' (Acts 2:11). In a world of chaos and confusion we look to the fulfilment of the ages when our Lord shall come in glory. When the Archbishop of Canterbury crowns the monarch in Westminster Abbey he uses the words that have been used in this ceremony for over 1,000 years: 'I give thee this crown to wear until he who reserves the right to wear it shall return.' Charles Wesley wrote some 6,500 hymns and the majority were about the second coming of Christ. One in every twenty-five verses of the Bible speak of it! The whole of history is pointing towards that great but awesome day.

In his novel *Till We Have Faces*, C S Lewis retells the myth of Cupid and Psyche with great spiritual insight. The coming of the god at the end of the book evokes the image of the second coming of Jesus:

Suddenly, from a strange look in Psyche's face . . . or from a glorious and awful deepening of the blue sky above us, or from a deep sigh uttered all around us by invisible lips, or from a deep, doubtful, quaking and surmise in my own heart, I knew that all this had been only a preparation. Some far greater matter was upon us. The voices spoke . . . They were awed and trembled. 'He is coming,' they said. 'The god is coming into his house. The god comes to judge Orual.' . . . The air was growing brighter and brighter about us; as if something had set it on fire. Each breath I drew let into me new terror, joy, overpowering sweetness. I was pierced through and through with the arrows of it. I was being unmade. I was no one. . . . The earth and stars and sun, all that was or will be, existed for his sake. And he was coming. The most dreadful, the most beautiful, the only dread and beauty there is, was coming. The pillars . . . flushed with his approach. I cast down my eyes.

The thought of his coming is one that fills us all with awe and trembling, but to the true believer it is a thought which thrills and gives hope. The true Church, the wise virgins, those who have kept their garments pure, await that hour with longing. The doctrine of the second coming has been neglected or made confusing and complicated by the Church. There are a multitude of doctrines and theories of pre-rapture, post- rapture, millenarianism, and so on. I try to keep the doctrine simple: he is coming, the Prince of peace is on his way, and he shall reign for ever and ever!

When Ron Allison was personal press secretary to the Queen he was asked by some reporters, 'What would be the best news you could ever receive?' He replied, to their amazement, 'That Jesus Christ had come again!' And that is the great news that we will one day hear:

'Behold, he cometh with clouds, and every eye shall see him' (Rev. 1:7)

Some council workers in Wiltshire were collecting refuge from outside a church and one of them noticed a poster which read: CHRIST IS ALIVE AND IS COMING AGAIN! He smiled sceptically and commented, 'He's a long time coming.' It is not easy to wait. It was not easy for the people of God when they wandered for 40 years in the wilderness, waiting for God to keep his word and lead them into the promised land. It is not easy for the persecuted believers in Communist countries. It is not easy for those who are in prison for the gospel's sake. It is not easy for those who are sick, who are suffering, who are bereaved, to wait patiently for his coming. But come he will: 'For the Lord himself shall descend from heaven with a shout . . . and the dead in Christ shall rise first. Then we which are alive and remain shall be caught up together with them in the clouds, to meet the Lord in the air, and so shall we ever be with the Lord' (1 Thess. 4:16-17).

Does that prospect thrill you? Or has the love of material things blunted your desire to see him? Have you stopped looking for his coming? Preachers, do you tell of his second coming or are you too taken up with other duties and doctrines? Friends, has your easy life-style blurred your view of the life to come? Have you become apathetic about God's judgment? Have you forgotten that he is coming soon?

Time is running out. The journey is nearly over. The gates of the celestial city will soon be in sight. The cry 'Jesus is coming!' will soon be 'Jesus has come!'. For those who are filled with the Spirit and walking in the light his coming will be their greatest joy. Let us shake off our lethargy, pray, work, and watch, for it is later than we think.

Years ago a train was travelling across the United States. It was before the days of air-conditioning; the train was hot and crowded; people were tired and irritable. A traveller noticed one little boy, travelling alone, who looked cool, calm, and happy. She asked him how he managed to seem so unruffled on such a long and uncomfortable journey and he replied, 'Well, you see, ma'am, I'm going to see my father when I get to Los Angeles.' We shall see our Heavenly Father when we get to our journey's end. This is the hope, the joy, the sustenance of the waiting believer.

I was recently in London with my wife and we went into the famous Harrods store in Knightsbridge. I noticed a sign over the main door, saying, 'Enter, you are entering into a new world'. Our King is returning and we will enter his new world! There we are promised life and liberty. On that day we shall arrive in the land of glorious and everlasting light where the darkness of night, the darkness of sin, the darkness of hell, the darkness of death, shall no longer grieve us. Then we shall see the fulfilment of the miracle of his second coming!

10: The Miracle of Christ's Challenge

'I want everything for God' – Watchman Nee

A new vicar came to a parish that I know which was beset by some long- standing and seemingly unresolvable problems. His predecessors in the area had all sought to get to the root of the problem and discuss it with the people involved. But this man ignored it completely and just kept on preaching week after week on the same theme: the need for everyone, himself included, to become more like Jesus. Some were offended, some accused him of 'hiding behind the Bible', some actually left the church. But he persevered. Slowly people began to catch his vision and the whole spirit of the parish changed. When the bishop visited it some years later he found a thriving, crowded, and caring church reaching out effectively to the community.

'The law of the Lord is perfect, converting the soul' (Ps. 19:7). He gives new direction to our attitudes and his intellect – if we will let him. Jesus describes people who resist conversion because they close their ears and eyes to him (Matt. 13:15). But see what the challenge of Jesus can do for those who are open to it: Peter, a rough fisherman, becomes so powerful a man of God that even his shadow heals the sick; the religious fanatic Saul becomes Paul, the lover of souls; a woman of ill repute becomes the messenger of the truth of God; a cold-hearted jailer becomes a gentle disciple. The same challenge is still being issued: 'Incline your ear, and come unto me: hear, and your soul shall live, and I will make an everlasting covenant with you' (Isa. 55:3). Accept my challenge, God says, and I will change you and keep on changing you. I see the challenge of Christ coming to us today in six ways.

1. The Challenge Of Christ's Lordship

Thomas, the doubter, at last recognised the Messiah and cried, 'My Lord and my God!' The first challenge for us is to recognise who Jesus is. Who is this Jesus? How can we describe him?

He is heaven's bread for earth's hunger.
He is heaven's water for earth's thirst.
He is heaven's clothing for earth's nakedness.
He is heaven's riches for earth's poverty.
He is heaven's light for earth's darkness.
He is heaven's grace for earth's guilt.
He is heaven's comfort for earth's sorrow.
He is heaven's glory for earth's shame.
He is heaven's wisdom for earth's foolishness.
He is heaven's peace for earth's strife.
He is heaven's forgiveness for earth's condemnation.

There is no one like Jesus. No one else has his love, his compassion, his power, his beauty. There is a story of an artist who was commisioned to paint the magnificent view from the windows of a monastery. On the first day the abbot came to see what he had done, but found he had not painted anything. It was the same on the second day, and the third, and finally the abbot asked when he intended to start. Looking out from the window at the beautiful scenery, the artist replied, 'I have started. In fact I have completed my picture, and tomorrow I shall begin putting it on the canvas.' He needed to feel the challenge of the task, to absorb the beauty and atmosphere of the place. We need to steep ourselves in the person of Jesus, to know his peace and his challenge. Corrie ten Boom has said, 'God has no problems with us – only plans for us.' We must get to know him and his plans for us. Our lives can be changed if we accept his challenge.

Once a shabbily dressed elderly man walked into a publisher's office in Moscow, clutching a manuscript. He handed it to the editor and asked if he might consider publishing it, but was told that they already had more manuscripts for consideration than they could cope with. The old man's face fell and, as he walked to the door, he said, 'I thought people wanted to read what I wrote.' 'What is your name?' the editor asked. 'Leo Tolstoy,' the old man replied as he walked out and vanished into the crowd. The editor rushed after him but it was too late. He had missed the chance of publishing the greatest Russian writer of all time! Oh, what chances we miss because we fail to recognise who Jesus is! How often we lose our way because we do not recognise his leading and guidance!

The former Bishop of Southwell, Dr Barry, said, 'Man is a well-fed anthill, all outside and no inside.' People are empty, lost, oppressed by loneliness and futility. The only answer is to heed the call of him who is the Word of God, incarnate, crucified, risen, and ascended. When we accept the challenge of the divine invitation we are accepting a Saviour who will be with us always, in all our problems, in all circumstances, wherever we go. He will never leave us or forsake us. He cannot disappoint us.

When we recognise who Jesus is our only response is to surrender ourselves completely, to abandon materialism and worldliness, and, like Isaac Watts, say:

Were the whole realm of nature mine,
That were an offering far too small,
Love so amazing, so divine,
Demands my heart, my life, my all.

With the acknowledgment of his Lordship, we are dedicating ourselves to complete commitment and discipleship. We cannot change the rules of entry into salvation. This taking up of the challenge of Christ in complete surrender has been described by Martin Luther as 'the joyful exchange' and by Billy Graham as 'the beautiful life'. Dr Sangster said that it is 'making Christ the King, not the President, for a king rules for life.'

Vance Havner once said, 'The tiniest post office can bear a letter that may wreck or bless a nation, and the simplest life can relay blessings that may rock a continent towards God.' The life that is once and for all surrendered, submitted, dedicated to the living God has the potential to change individuals and whole societies for good. Let us take up that challenge and seek the God-filled life, the God-filled walk. King Saul's admission was, 'I have played the fool, and have erred exceedingly' (1 Sam. 26:21). This is the tragic confession we all have to make. But what joy if we can at last say with the other Saul, 'For me to live is Christ, and to die is gain' (Phil. 1:21)!

2. The Challenge Of The Holy Spirit

On a Saturday night many years ago when I was a young man I went to the Sunday School hall to fetch some materials for my lesson the next morning. I had not realised that there was a meeting going on in the hall – a meeting for those who were seeking the power of the Holy Spirit. When I saw all the people in the hall I was about to leave but the preacher called me in and I was too embarrassed to say that I had not intended to come to the meeting. I allowed myself to be led to the front of the hall, where I sat in prayer. Then the preacher laid hands on me and immediately I realised that I *did* want more from God. I just threw myself upon the Lord and in a minute or so I burst into a heavenly language that I had never learned. Such power, joy, and fire spread through my soul that I was drunk with the glory of it. My wife, who had come looking for me, found me quite oblivious of all my surroundings, lost in the joy of the Lord. She had to help me onto the bus and the conductor assumed I was drunk. 'Yes,' Lilian told him, 'He's drunk on a wine that's 2,000 years old!' 'It's got some power then!' the conductor replied.

The power of the Holy Spirit has been with me since I accepted God's challenge that night. I have needed many infillings since but I am still under the mighty influence of that blessing.

Almost exactly 24 years after that night I was preaching in a tent to nearly 3,000 Zulu people in a shanty town in Natal. There was no church in the town but Charismatic Christians had erected this tent and had been holding meetings there every night for eight weeks. No one in that vast crowd had been a Christian for longer than eight weeks. I preached the gospel and many found Jesus. A blind man had his sight restored.

Then I told them about the Trinity, which I explained by comparing it to an egg which has three parts – shell, white, and yolk – yet is one. I told them that God was one but had three persons and that the Holy Spirit is the third person in the Trinity. I asked how many of them would like to be filled with the Holy Spirit, and most put up their hands. I told them to breathe in the Spirit and then speak, not in English, not in their own language, but in the heavenly language God would give them. After a few minutes I heard a beautiful sound rising from hundreds of lips, a heavenly language as from a myriad of angels. The sound grew and grew; 500 must have been filled with the Holy Spirit that night. These people who had only recently heard the gospel and only that night heard of the Holy Spirit were filled with his power, their faces shining with the glory of God. I felt like Peter in the house of Cornelius!

A friend of mine is so full of Holy Ghost power that people occasionally fall back in his presence. He was in Africa and went into a furniture shop to buy some chairs. When the assistant saw him he immediately said, 'I can see Jesus in your eyes.' Then he fell to the floor weeping and begged my friend to tell him about Jesus. My friend led him to the Lord there and then on the floor of the furniture shop. Walking home later he was talking to the Lord and asked him, 'What did that man mean, Lord, when he said he could see Jesus in my eyes?' The Lord told him, 'Why, I live in you, don't I? All I was doing was looking out of the windows!' My friend had taken up the challenge of the Holy Spirit and proved that it worked.

We must tell the world that the anointing of the Holy Spirit brings new and victorious life. I once held a crusade in a hall which was just opposite a huge poster advertising beer: DOUBLE DIAMOND WORKS

WONDERS EVERY NIGHT. I put up a poster outside the crusade hall: D.A. WORKS WONDERS EVERY NIGHT HERE. The crowds were drawn in by curiosity and I explained to a packed congregation what it meant: 'Double anointing works wonders.' And indeed it did. The challenge of the divine power of the Spirit was accepted by hundreds and many received a mighty baptism of power.

3. The Challenge Of Prayer

A professor was climbing the Weisshorn with an experienced Swiss guide. When they reached the top the professor stood looking at the magnificent view when suddenly the guide pulled him down, calling, 'Quick, down on your knees!' 'A wind is coming,' he explained, 'and the only safe place is on your knees.' We are on the edge of a precipice today and our only place of safety is at God's feet in prayer.

Dr Yonggi Cho, when asked what was the way forward for the Church today, replied, 'Pray, pray, pray!' Only through prayer can we know God. Double your prayer time and you double the blessings in your life. We must cast off our sluggishness and find time for prayer. Throughout the Old and New Testaments we can see how the servants of God have sought him in prayer. And his word is still the same to the Church today: Seek and ye shall find.

Before a large crusade we often spend the night in prayer, and what a difference it makes! Some people in a little church in West Wales recently prayed all night that I would accept an invitation to hold a mission in their area and that God would visit and bless them. When I heard of their prayers my heart was lifted and the Lord led me to accept the invitation. Revival blessing broke out there in a remarkable way: hundreds were converted, and many were healed.

Prayer brings a sobering to God's people, taking us down from the 'froth and bubble', leading us to the fruits, not just the gifts, of the Holy Spirit. When we open our whole being to God we are forced into honesty. I see the Church as a praying body, an army of earnest beseechers pulling down strongholds, a militant force kicking down the gates of hell. Prayer is not just one of the elements of Church life but its primary force. Look at the power of the church meetings in the Book of Acts: prayer is seen against a background of action, and its effects are unpredictable and dynamic.

How sad that for so many people the prayer meeting has become a boring part of church routine. The challenge of learning to pray honestly is exciting but many have lost sight of this because of the stagnant prayer heard so often in church meetings. Many prayers are directed not to God, but to the congregation; some people pray in the same words every time so they sound like a record playing; some turn their prayer into advice to the pastors or criticism of the way the church is progressing. It is time to bury that kind of meeting, which can kill the effect of real prayer. We need honest, earnest passionate prayer, telling God everything that is in our hearts.

In the final secret message received from the saintly Watchman Nee from prison in China, just before he died, were these words:

Ask! Since God is always there in the unseen, there is no situation on this earth in which you and I are powerless to do anything. Whether shackled by foes, or hampered by circumstances, whether totally paralysed or walled up in solitary darkness, we can pray,

121

we can appeal to him, we can ask, we can surely
appeal to him, we can ask, we shall surely receive.
God will act if we will but go on asking. . .

Through the challenge of prayer the Church has an
outstanding future. It can enable us to defeat the powers
of darkness and win the day!

4. The Challenge Of Revival

The Hebrew word *hecheyah* is used some 40 times in the
Old Testament to mean 'revive' or 'restore to life'. It is
used of the great Old Testament revivals, such as those
under Nehemiah and Ezra. Psalm 5:6 says, 'Revive us
again that your people may rejoice in you.' In Habbakuk
Chapter 3 we have the prophet's famous prayer for
revival: 'O Lord, revive thy work in the midst of the
years' (Hab.3:2). In the New Testament the Greek word
anazopureo is used, for example in Paul's advice to
Timothy to 'stir up the gift of God that is in you' (2
Tim. 1:6), with the sense of 'rekindle', 'fan the embers',
'bring the fire back to life'.

What is revival? Tozer said it was 'that which changes
the moral climate of a community'; Havner calls it 'the
saints getting back to normal'; Arthur Wallis has said
that it is 'such a manifestation and working of God, that
human personalities are overshadowed, man is in the
background, and God is taking the field.' Revival is
more than successful evangelism: in evangelism we are
working for God, but in revival God is working on behalf
of us.

In revival the righteousness of God is made manifest
in events beyond human control: in the deliverance from
demons, in miracles, and wonderful conversions. All over
the world I have witnessed the phenomenon of a healing

122

mission moving into a sovereign and divine visitation, unorganised and flowing straight from the throne of God.

I hope for and long to see revival in Britain but there seem to be special problems here. People are so easily satisfied. As soon as a church sees a few people saved, they think they can relax for the next couple of years; people speak in tongues a little, see a few healings and they think they now have everything. Some years ago a church in England wrote to me saying that they did not need any more evangelistic or healing missions. They had reached a congregation of 100 and did not need any more people – this in a town with a population of 75,000! More than one church has asked me to postpone a planned visit for a year or two because my last visit had left them with so many converts they could not manage any more new people for a while. How pathetic! How sadly lacking in passion and vision!

God wants to raise up a people who have persistence and zeal, born again, sanctified people who long for revival and are prepared to pay the price in dedication. Revival does not come from the diluted, feeble form of Christianity found in so many churches; revival comes with nights of prayer and fasting. God will move to bless the sincere, soul-seeking, prayer-hungry heart.

What are the marks of revival? It comes suddenly as it did ten years ago in a prayer meeting in a little chapel in west Cornwall when the Holy Ghost shook the building and the resulting revival saw churches planted and great works of God in that area. Revival brings repentance, weeping, confession, and joy, miracles and the defeat of evil. In revival God meets material needs in a way that nullifies both atheistic Marxism and greedy capitalism. The hungry are fed, widows and orphans cared for, the gospel spread, and God's covenant fulfilled. In revival the lordship of Christ is made manifest to the world.

5. The Challenge Of Restoration

We live in days of undisciplined, unfruitful, and defeatist believers. God cannot use a weak, anaemic body which has lost its own moral moorings and can give no inspiration and encouragement to the world. He needs a harmonious people who are following his scriptural plan. What a challenge to us – to rebuild, restructure, restore his Church!

By *restoration* I am not suggesting any new denomination or new group with some new theory or theology. I mean the restoration of 'all things' (Matt. 17:11) that must come to the body before the final outpouring of the Spirit upon all flesh. God is raising a remnant, a people ready for conquest. But the first need is for personal restoration. We each need restoring to God's wholeness, a deepening of faith, a fresh appreciation of all that is ours in Christ.

God wants to lead his Church from condemnation, lifelessness, and apathy to freedom, dedication, and power. He wants a purified, victorious Church built on his word. We must seek to bring our churches, fellowships, and house groups into line with his teaching, to establish a powerful, invigorated covenant Church. I heard of a church which cancelled its meeting one winter's day. The weather had prevented the preacher from getting there and they thought they could not have the meeting without him. Some churches are like the old solo planes of the First World War, where one man had to do all the work. Tony Morton likened the restored body to 'a jumbo jet taking off, whole communities becoming full of power . . . and rising together, everyone participating . . .'

The restored Church has turned its back on cold, formal tradition and is pulsating with energy, joy, and the power of God's promises. It reflects the glory and authority of God, equipped and walking in his way, accepting his challenges, reaching the world with salvation and hope. *I urge you to find your place and part in this Resurrection cmmunity.*

6. The Challenge Of Evangelism

Jesus tells us to 'go and tell', to be 'fishers of men'. God is seeking lost men and women all over the world and the gospel must be preached everywhere until everyone has had a chance of salvation. God gives us the challenge of rescuing a lost world. The German religious reformer Zinzendorf urged his followers with the cry; 'Tell them about the Lamb of God until you can tell them no more.' Bob Geldof inspired millions to give to the famine victims of Ethiopia with the rallying cry, 'People are dying - what are you doing to help?' We can spiritualise these words: people's souls are dying — what are we doing to rescue them?

The Lord is stirring his people. As I have travelled the world I have been encouraged by what I have seen: from Austria to Korea, from South Africa to New Zealand, hundreds are being converted, churches are being planted, leaders established.

So many men and women over the years have responded to God's challenge to evangelism and have brought new life and hope where there was darkness and despair. My own call came when I was first asked to preach at a healing crusade. I was a substitute; I had been asked because the preacher they had originally wanted had been unable to come. I was full of anxiety and trepidation but there were blessings that night and my courage was roused to accept God's challenge and follow step by step along the pathway that Christ was revealing to me. This has led to a world-wide ministry and the joy of seeing the sick, sinful, defeated, and depressed become healthy, pure, victorious, and happy!

Corrie ten Boom once said, 'There is only one way to answer the challenges of Christ to us, and that is surrender.' God is calling us to a new devotion, humility and dedication, to surrender our lives to him. He will equip us for the work he calls us to – his yoke is easy and his burden is light.

A small boy, walking along the beach of an English seaside resort, picked up one starfish after another as he sauntered along, throwing each one of the dying creatures back into the sea. His uncle laughed at his efforts to save them in the scorching heat. 'There are thousands of starfish as far as you can go along this beach' he chuckled. 'By the time the tide gets in, they will all be dead.' Then the small boy stopped, lifted one up in his hand, and said seriously, 'Uncle, to this one starfish it makes all the difference in the world that I have saved him.'

Jesus has rescued you. He makes all the difference to us. He has regenerated, chosen, lifted us to the dazzling heights of splendour. Now, answer His challenge and He will catapult you into the orbit of the miraculous, and you will discover the greatest miracle of all is our Shepherd, Sufferer and Saviour. Our Rock, Restorer and Redeemer. Our Prince, Priest and Purifier, Our King and Lord – Jesus Christ.

If you wish to receive *regular information* about *new books*, please send your name and address to:

London Bible Warehouse
PO Box 123
Basingstoke
Hants RG23 7NL

Name _____

Address _____

_____

_____

_____

I am especially interested in:
- [ ] Biographies
- [ ] Fiction
- [ ] Christian living
- [ ] Issue related books
- [ ] Academic books
- [ ] Bible study aids
- [ ] Children's books
- [ ] Music
- [ ] Other subjects

Other Marshall Pickering Paperbacks

JOIN THE COMPANY

Adrian Plass

When TV viewers in the south tune into 'Company', they can eavesdrop on a few friends enjoying some late night conversation around a kitchen table. For Adrian Plass, the programme is a landmark in his Christian life. With disarming frankness and irresistible humour, he unfolds his own story and that of some of the programme's memorable guests, such as David Watson, cleaning lady Jo Williams and Auschwitz survivor, Rabbi Hugo Grynn.

WHEN YOU PRAY

Reginald East

Spiritual renewal has awakened in many Christians a deeper longing to know God more intimately. Prayer is the place where we personally meet God, yet it is often treated simply as the means for making requests for our needs, and offering out stilted, dutiful thanks. In this practical guide to prayer, Reginald East shows how we can establish a prayer relationship with God which is both spiritually and emotionally satisfying. Through understanding God and ourselves better, prayer can truly become an encounter with God, where we relax into Him, enjoy Him, listen as well as talk to Him and adventure into discovering His heart of love.